Australian Edition

Getting Started in Bookkeeping

FOR

DUMMIES®

Australian Edition

Getting Started in Bookkeeping

FOR

DUMMIES®

by Veechi Curtis

WILEY

Wiley Publishing Australia Pty Ltd

Getting Started in Bookkeeping For Dummies®

Australian Edition published by
Wiley Publishing Australia Pty Ltd
42 McDougall Street
Milton, Qld 4064
www.dummies.com

Copyright © 2010 Wiley Publishing Australia Pty Ltd

The moral rights of the author have been asserted.

National Library of Australia
Cataloguing-in-Publication data:

Author:	Curtis, Veechi.
Title:	Getting Started in Bookkeeping For Dummies/Veechi Curtis.
Edition:	Australian ed.
ISBN:	978 1 74246 874 7 (pbk.)
Notes:	Includes index.
Subjects:	Bookkeeping — Australia.
Dewey Number:	657.2

Cover image: © iStockphoto.com/Uyen Le

Typeset by diacriTech, Chennai, India

Printed in China by
Printplus Limited

10 9 8 7 6 5 4 3 2 1

About the Author

Veechi Curtis has a degree in Accountancy and Business Management from Charles Sturt University, and has worked as a business consultant for more than 13 years, including several years running a contract bookkeeping service. As a journalist, she has written for many publications including *Australian PC World*, *Australian Personal Computer* and *CCH Australia Limited*, and has also been a columnist for *The Sydney Morning Herald*.

Veechi is also the author of *Small Business For Dummies*, *MYOB Software For Dummies* and *QuickBooks QB^i For Dummies* and co-author of *Bookkeeping For Dummies* and *Business Plans For Dummies*.

Veechi has three children and lives with her husband in the beautiful Blue Mountains of New South Wales. Feel free to send Veechi a message, or ask a question about this book, via her website at www.veechicurtis.com.au.

Author's Acknowledgements

Veechi would like to thank Andrew White of Benetatos White
for his help with legal questions. Thanks also to the John Wiley
editorial team: Rev Mengle, Hannah Bennett, Jen Bingham,
Bronwyn Duhigg, Caroline Hunter and Gabrielle Packman.

Last but not least, thanks to my very silly and wonderful family,
who provide me with all the inspiration I could ever need.

Publisher's Acknowledgements

We're proud of this book; please send us your comments through our online registration form located at http://dummies.custhelp.com.

Some of the people who helped bring this book to market include the following:

Acquisitions, Editorial and Media Development

Acquisitions Editor: Rebecca Crisp

Editorial Manager: Hannah Bennett

Production

Graphics: Wiley Art Studio

Cartoons: Glen Lumsden

Proofreader: Liz Goodman

Indexer: Veechi Curtis

The authors and publisher would like to thank the following copyright holders, organisations and individuals for their permission to reproduce copyright material in this book.

- MYOB Australia: screen captures from MYOB reproduced with permission. Copyright © 2010 MYOB Technology Pty Ltd
- Reckon Limited: Copyright © 2010 Intuit Inc. All rights reserved
- Xero: Screenshot on **page 64** reproduced with permission from Xero
- Microsoft Corporation: MS Excel screenshots reprinted by permission from Microsoft Corporation

Every effort has been made to trace the ownership of copyright material. Information that will enable the publisher to rectify any error or omission in subsequent editions will be welcome. In such cases, please contact the Permissions Section of John Wiley & Sons Australia, Ltd.

Contents at a Glance

Table of Contents

. . . .

Introduction

● ●

I first started working as a bookkeeper in my late teens, doing handwritten books in leather-bound journals down by the docks in my hometown of Edinburgh, Scotland. Later, I emigrated to Australia, where I got a job working as a bookkeeper in the Blue Mountains west of Sydney. There I worked with first-generation accounting software, substituting the peace of those inky journals for a battle of wills (myself versus the computer) that required a bizarre mixture of programming skills and native cunning.

By my late twenties, I had a small business of my own, employing four staff and offering bookkeeping services to local businesses. I finished a degree in accounting (which contributed surprisingly little to my bookkeeping expertise), and started writing for magazines and newspapers reviewing accounting software. In the following years, I wrote a fair few *For Dummies* titles, including *MYOB Software For Dummies* and *QuickBooks For Dummies*.

Even with all this experience behind me, I was in a bit of a quandary as to how to structure the project that you have in your hands right now — *Getting Started in Bookkeeping For Dummies*. I didn't want a dull, theoretical approach that laboured on about debits and credits, but nor did I want to write an accounting software how-to guide. Instead, I've tried to strike a balance, with a book that explains the principles of bookkeeping in the context of doing business in the 21st century.

About This Book

This book talks about getting started with bookkeeping, explaining accounting concepts such as debits and credits, the difference between an asset and a liability, and how expenses are different from income. I also explore the pros and cons of the different ways of bookkeeping — are you best to do books by hand, use a spreadsheet or purchase accounting software?

I explain how to record expenses (the scary bit), how to keep track of income (much more fun) and how to balance your bank account. Hopefully, these skills combined can help you sleep well at night, with no counting of sheep required.

How to Use This Book

Getting Started in Bookkeeping For Dummies isn't a gripping novel to be read from cover to cover. This book is designed (all 10 bite-sized chunks) so you can pick it up at any point and just start reading.

If you're a business owner and you're looking to set up a bookkeeping system for your own business, I recommend you read Chapters 1, 2 and 4 before doing much else. If you want to know more about recording income and expenses, hop to Chapters 6 and 7. And for the serious stuff — reconciling bank accounts and understanding financial statements — make your way to Chapters 8 and 9.

Foolish Assumptions

Because I'm so blindingly sensible, I don't make any foolish assumptions about you, dear reader. I don't assume that you have any bookkeeping experience or even that you've worked in a business before (although it's possible, of course, that you're a bookkeeper extraordinaire with 30 years' experience under your belt). All I assume is that you are at least vaguely interested in bookkeeping and the results that the process yields.

How This Book is Organised

This book is split into four parts.

Part 1: First Steps

In Chapter 1, I talk about training as a bookkeeper and what skills you need. I also explore different approaches to bookkeeping and give a quick rundown on the whole bookkeeping life cycle. In Chapters 2 and 3, I explain bookkeeping concepts that apply to all businesses, large or small.

Part II: Forming a Plan

The second part of this book focuses on systems: Chapter 4 explores why all but the rarest of bookkeeping situations can benefit from accounting software; and Chapter 5 looks at GST, and how you deal with GST on everyday transactions.

Part III: Recording Day-to-Day Transactions

In Chapters 6 and 7, I explain how to record income and expenses, and how to allocate everyday transactions. By the time Chapter 8 rolls around, you're ready to start balancing your work and reconciling your bank account to check that you haven't made any mistakes.

If you're anxious about working with financial reports, don't be. I devote all of Chapter 9 to understanding Balance Sheets and Profit & Loss reports.

Part IV: The Part of Tens

The Part of Tens is my favourite part of any Dummies title. Chapter 10 offers tactics for getting customers to pay on time.

Icons Used in This Book

Throughout this book you'll find icons in the margins to help you navigate through the text. Here's what these icons mean:

 This icon flags where I explain how to put bookkeeping theory into practice using accounting software.

 Want to be streets ahead of the competition? Then look for this handy icon.

 You'll find this icon next to stuff relating to GST or taxation (ah, such fascinating topics).

So people think that accountants and bookkeepers are boring? Another myth just waiting to be busted.

 Tie a knot in your hankie, pin an egg-timer to your shirt but, whatever you do, don't forget these little nuggets.

 This icon points the way to doing your job better, faster and smarter.

 Real-life stories from bookkeepers who've been there provide all the history lessons you could ever want.

 A pitfall for the unwary. Read these warnings carefully (then you can't say no-one told you . . .).

Part I
First Steps

Glenn Lumsden

*'Representing Australasia, Debbie Wilson
will be performing a double-entry
transferrance to general ledger
with debit and credit.'*

In this part ...

*B*ookkeepers provide the life-giving oxygen for everyday commerce. Without bookkeepers, businesses wouldn't know if they're making or losing money, getting ahead or falling behind. Without bookkeepers, the world would likely grind to a halt and cease to do business.

In the first part of this book, I talk about what makes a good bookkeeper, daring to suggest that attitude is just as important as a string of qualifications. I help you get started on this whole bookkeeping game, building your first custom-fit chart of accounts.

I also show no fear and dive into the debits and credits of double-entry accounting. Is it indecent that a person could have so much fun? Maybe — but you're just the person for the job.

Chapter 1

Introducing the Bookkeeping Game

- -

In This Chapter

▶ Introducing the bookkeeping life cycle — from chrysalis to butterfly

▶ Matching bookkeeping systems to the game in hand

▶ Pulling together a record-keeping system

▶ Developing a bookkeeper's mindset

▶ Finding out whether you need to get more training

- -

*I*n some ways, bookkeeping is like cooking up a fine meal. The process of washing and chopping and steaming and frying isn't much to write home about. What makes everything worthwhile is the outcome: The hot taste in your mouth, the warm feeling in your belly. A good bottle of red simply adds to the fun.

In the same way, adding up receipts and paying bills isn't the most exciting activity in the world. What brings the buzz to bookkeeping are the results: An organised office, cash in the bank and a set of financial reports that help a business succeed. After all, without a Profit & Loss report, how does a business know how it's doing? And without a Balance Sheet, how can a business owner gauge their personal worth?

In this chapter, I explore the qualities of a good bookkeeper: Not just someone who can record transactions accurately, but someone who cares about the financial statements that they generate. I also talk about training as a bookkeeper and what skills you need, about setting up systems, keeping good records, and about understanding the bookkeeping life cycle from go to whoa.

Understanding the Bookkeeping Life Cycle

Bookkeeping has a certain anachronistic quality to it, especially if you look beyond the glitzy buttons in your accounting software and start getting familiar with some of the terminology. But like many things that stem from the past, bookkeeping is a deeply logical process that flows beautifully from one stage to the next.

The essence of bookkeeping — and the beginning of any bookkeeping entry — is a *transaction*. You already know instinctively what a transaction is: The sale of goats, the purchase of sheep or the exchange of shining gold coins.

Your gig as a bookkeeper is to record every itsy bitsy transaction that takes place, and you do this using a *journal*. This journal may be a traditional ledger book, smelling of ink, sweat and musty leather. More pragmatically, this journal can take the form of a spreadsheet or a data-entry window in an accounting software program.

Whenever you log transactions in this faithful journal, you're making a *journal entry*. As you record each journal entry, you have the nail-biting decision of what *account* this entry goes to. If this transaction is an expense, for example, is it for money-lending fees, servant's quarters or water-hauling?

At the end of each month, you total the columns in each journal (if you can't find an abacus, then a calculator will do). Using the principles of double-entry bookkeeping, you then transfer these totals to the *general ledger* (a great fat tome that summarises the entries from all the other journals). This transfer process is called *posting*, and happens automatically if you use accounting software.

Last but not least, you draw up a report using the final balances from the general ledger, creating a document called a *trial balance*. The amounts in the trial balance form the basis for key pillars of wisdom such as the *Profit & Loss report*, which summarises income, expense and net profit, and the *Balance Sheet report*, which summarises the value of assets, liabilities and equity. (Again, if you use accounting software, these reports are generated automatically.)

The next day dawns and you, the bookkeeper, are to be found at your desk once more, recording transactions in your faithful journals. And so there you have it: The life cycle of bookkeeping in a nutshell, with a distinctly historical twist, starting with a simple transaction and culminating in a set of financial statements that let everyone know what's what.

Figuring How Often to Do the Deed

So how often do you need to do this whole bookkeeping game? On the one hand, you don't want to get so behind that you can't produce reports or see what customers owe you, but on the other hand, you don't want to overdo things, working on your books so often that you record only one or two transactions each time.

While you're of course free to chart your own course, here's a look at the pluses and pitfalls of the two most common methods: Doing your books once every few months (see the next section, 'Working with a shoebox') and doing your books on a regular basis (see the section 'Doing the books as you go' later in the chapter).

Working with a shoebox

Shoebox accounting brings a comfortable chaos to any business. As the financial year ticks by, the owner of the business dumps all bank statements, receipts and supplier bills in a messy heap somewhere. Once a year, usually days before a tax return is due, either the business owner or an unfortunate bookkeeper retrieves this unhappy heap, and attempts to put it in some kind of order.

I've been the unfortunate bookkeeper in this situation many a time. Admittedly very few shoeboxes, but instead, piles of dog-eared receipts in scrappy manila folders, old fruit boxes, tattered briefcases and one time, a complete timber drawer straight out of the client's desk.

Shoebox accounting has its advantages:

- ✔ You can ignore the drudgery of year-round bookkeeping, a tactic that suits the ostriches of this world.
- ✔ Bookkeeping is sometimes a relatively swift process, because you churn through a whole year's transactions in one hit.

A cautionary tale

When my husband and I first started living together, I didn't dare interfere with his trusted shoebox system of bookkeeping. I bit my lip as I observed him stuffing unopened bank and credit card statements into the bulging drawers of the office desk, and scarcely muttered a word as he deposited customer cheques into his bank account without even keeping a record of who had paid him, and what for.

A year or so ticked by before my husband delicately suggested that in the spirit of relationship bonding, I might like to do his books for him (adding that his tax return had been due the previous month). Sure, I replied, with my inveterate Pollyanna 'can do' attitude.

It was bad, really bad. 'What was this debit for in your bank statement?' I'd ask. He'd shrug. I'd shrug back. Another tax deduction lost. 'Don't you have a single receipt for a year's worth of petrol?' I'd ask. 'No, I hate fiddly little bits of paper', he'd reply.

But the sting came when I got to his credit card statements. 'What's this debit for $120 every month for a year, made in US dollars?' 'Nothing to do with me', he replied. I queried the debits with the bank, who confirmed they were a scam, but because too much time had elapsed before me querying the transactions, a refund was impossible.

'I told you so', I announced triumphantly. 'That's okay, darling', he replied. 'I'm fine for you to do my books all the time. You'll find the paperwork in that drawer over there.' I remain unconvinced as to whether this is an improvement in our married life, or not.

And disadvantages ...

✔ You miss out on the benefits of doing your books, such as up-to-date financial reports or budgets.

✔ If any bank statements are missing, by the time you realise, you usually can't view the transactions on the internet (because most banks only go back 120 days with online transaction listings).

By the time you do the books, you've forgotten what some of the transactions are, so you waste hours trying to do things like match up receipts against miscellaneous electronic debits from your bank account.

 In short, I recommend shoebox accounting only for the smallest of small businesses, such as a hobby business, or a business with no GST, no wages, few bills and irregular income.

Doing the books as you go

Most businesses do most of the day-to-day bookkeeping as transactions occur. If you use accounting software, every time you make a sale to a customer, you record the sale in your books. Voilà, the bookkeeping for this transaction is complete. Similarly, when you receive a payment, you record the transaction against outstanding customer invoices and, in the process, you complete the bookkeeping for the transaction.

I find that most bookkeepers arrive at a certain rhythm, a rhythm that's determined by how often a business needs to pay bills, issue customer statements or generate reports. Read through the different activities below and see whether you can pick up any tips about how to organise your time.

Record sales transactions once and once only

Here's my number one rule: Generating a sales invoice and recording this sale in your books should be one and the same activity. You can streamline your business processes in a number of ways, including the following:

 ✔ **Don't record sales in a word processor:** Almost all businesses generate invoices on their computer nowadays. If you use accounting software to do your books, then use your accounting software to record sales. Don't be tempted to use a word-processing program to generate sales, even if the colours and flexibility of word processing seem attractive. Spend the time customising the sales templates in your accounting software instead.

✔ **If you're a retailer, integrate your point-of-sale system and your accounting software:** If you integrate your point-of-sale system with your accounting software, daily sales totals and stock movements carry across automatically from one system to another. In other words, as soon as you make a sale in the shop, the bookkeeping for this sale is taken care of. Ah, the wonders of modern life.

✔ **Ditch handwritten docket books:** If you write invoices by hand because you're out in the field, consider switching to a smartphone (such as a BlackBerry or an Apple iPhone) that integrates with your accounting software. This way, you can generate invoices on the spot and then synchronise these sales with your accounting software when you return to the office.

Pay supplier accounts in batches

Checking supplier bills, balancing supplier statements and paying accounts are some of the most time-consuming parts of a bookkeeper's job.

My main tip for bookkeepers is to set a schedule for bill payments, then stick to it. For example, if you have weekly accounts, then set one day per week where you settle these bills. If you have monthly accounts, set aside one day per month (usually a day that falls between the 20th and the last day of the month).

Avoid paying bills in dribs and drabs, and invest time to negotiate arrangements for suppliers wanting cash on delivery.

Use software to manage employee pays

If you have employees, chances are you already have payroll software. If so, record wages straight into your payroll software, using the software to record start and finish times, and to calculate tax, superannuation and print payslips. This way, the very process of calculating and generating employees' pay means that the bookkeeping for payroll is complete.

I occasionally come across businesses that still maintain a handwritten wages book, where employees sign for their pay each week, because the business owner operates under the false impression that employees have to sign for their pay. That's not true! There's no legal obligation that requires employees to sign for wages every week. If someone is going to dispute receiving a certain amount, they can do so whether or not they have signed.

Reconcile often, reconcile well

Reconciling bank accounts is one of the core tasks for any bookkeeper (and a process that I talk about in much more detail in Chapter 8). Put simply, a bank reconciliation is when you match everything that's on your bank statement against everything in your books, double-checking that your work is correct.

Always reconcile the main business cheque account before chasing customers for money, generating activity statements or GST returns, or printing management reports. For small- to medium-sized businesses, this means you probably reconcile accounts once every week or fortnight; for micro businesses, once a month probably does just fine.

Use the rhythm method

For small businesses, try to establish a regular rhythm for when you do your books, and if possible, schedule as many bookkeeping activities as possible onto the same day per week. For example, set the same day every week to record both pay and weekly supplier payments.

If you find it hard to stick to a routine and find yourself doing books in dribs and drabs whenever you have a free moment, consider delegating the bookkeeping to somebody else.

Many small businesses have a book-keeper who comes in once per week for a half day just to do the whole bookkeeping function.

Devising a Record-keeping System

Organising business paperwork into some kind of order is a crucial part of a bookkeeper's job. Hey, you may think to yourself, don't I just whack stuff in a folder in date order and forget about it? Well, you could, but chances are you would waste heaps of time in the coming months looking for things. You're best to devise a system that keeps records as accessible as possible.

Filing that needle in the haystack

What goes where? Here are some ideas:

- **Cash receipts:** Ah, petty cash. How you organise receipts depends on what method you use. A fair slab of Chapter 6 is devoted to this topic.

- **Copies of customer invoices:** If you use accounting software, you don't need to keep a printed copy of customer invoices, because you already have a copy in your accounting file. (My own proviso is you must ensure you have a rock solid backup system in place.) If you generate customer invoices using any other system (such as a word processor or docket book), then make sure to keep a copy of each invoice, filed in invoice number order.

- **Credit card or EFTPOS receipts:** If you receive a receipt for something paid by credit card (a tank of fuel for example), then you need to keep this receipt for tax purposes, as a credit card statement by itself isn't enough of a record to satisfy a tax audit. However, you don't really need to refer to this receipt again for bookkeeping purposes (most bookkeepers prefer to record credit card transactions by working through the credit card statement, rather than sorting through a pile of dockets). I tend to stuff credit card and EFTPOS receipts in my wallet, then tip them out once a month and stuff them into an envelope labelled 'Credit card and EFTPOS receipts'. However, if you're doing the books for a business where a lot of employees have corporate credit card accounts, ask each employee to supply you with receipts and then staple these receipts onto the back of each credit card statement.

- **Electronic payments:** If you pay accounts electronically, then check whether your internet banking provides a history of past payments that goes back at least

12 months. If not, I suggest you keep a copy of the payment confirmation messages. Probably the simplest approach is to print the confirmation message and file in date order in a ring binder. (Alternatively, if you're a tech-head like me, you can copy and paste the confirmation message into an email message, email it to yourself, and then file this email in an Outlook folder called Electronic Payments.)

✔ **Paid supplier bills:** I prefer to file supplier bills alphabetically by name, and within each name, in date order. With my own business, I have two lever arch folders with coloured dividers for each letter of the alphabet. The bills for each supplier are grouped together, with the most recent bill at the top. At the end of each financial year I move the bills into an archive box, and start afresh with a new folder.

✔ **Unpaid supplier bills:** The simplest system is to pop unpaid supplier bills in manila folders awaiting payment, with one folder for weekly accounts, and another for monthly accounts. After you pay a bill, transfer it to the 'Paid' folder.

Give bookkeepers a chance

Are you a business owner who employs a bookkeeper? If so, I can suggest a few tips to help your bookkeeper be as efficient as possible.

My number one tip is to keep your personal and business expenses separate and, if you don't have a separate personal bank account, get one now. (It can cost a bookkeeper hours every month identifying what's business and what's personal, and separating the two.) Second, keep receipts for all your expenses, and try to separate cash receipts from EFTPOS or credit card receipts. Third, help your bookkeeper organise bills and receipts — splash out on a few ring-binder folders and devise a record-keeping system where you can both find stuff.

Fourth, before your bookkeeper arrives, spend time gathering together all the necessary paperwork. Print out bank statements if they're missing, and write explanations on the bank statements against any amounts where it's not clear what the expense was for.

Lastly, try to stick around while your bookkeeper is working, so you can answer questions as they crop up. Work together to draw up a schedule of deadlines for the year (GST reports, tax returns and so on), so that your bookkeeper can plan ahead to meet this schedule.

With my business, I organise all my utility bills (gas, electricity, phone and so on) so that I receive the bill by email, and when the bill falls due, my business account is debited automatically. When I receive a utility bill, I quickly check the total and then archive this email in a special Outlook folder called Tax Invoices. I don't worry about printing the bill — in the event of an audit, I still have an electronic copy. I simply make sure that I back up my Outlook data every week (something that's a good idea in any case).

Deciding what to keep and for how long

You need to keep your business records for a full five years after your tax return is lodged. However, the legal statute of limitations says that you can be sued for a transaction up to seven years afterwards, so for most transactions, seven years is actually a safer bet than five. As well as this, any records relating to capital gains tax may need to be kept for even longer because you may need to substantiate the purchase price of assets purchased years, or even decades, earlier.

If you use accounting software, remember to archive your company file at the end of each financial year onto a CD or removable hard drive. Store these archives away from the office and, if you use a password to get into your accounting file, write this password down, maybe even on the CD itself. (Years ago, I remember assisting with an audit where the client needed to show wage records for the past five years. She had all her backup CDs close to hand, but guess what? She'd forgotten what her password used to be. What a nightmare.)

Developing an Attitude

Over the years, I've worked with and taught lots of bookkeepers: Young and old, qualified and unqualified. Some scarily cocky, others achingly unsure, a few startlingly beautiful and many more rather careworn.

So what separates a good bookkeeper from a bad bookkeeper? Being young and beautiful doesn't help much, that's for sure (at least not with bookkeeping). Qualifications help, but aren't the whole story either. Nay, I reckon what separates the wheat from the chaff is *attitude*.

A good bookkeeper cares when something doesn't balance; gets upset when stuff goes missing, and goes a tad apoplectic at the sight of a disorganised office. A bookkeeper cares that the financial statements make sense, and feels responsible when it comes to getting customers to pay on time. Good bookkeepers, in other words, are worth their weight in gold.

Convince yourself this stuff matters

If you're already a bona fide, serious bookkeeper, you probably know that doing the books is a vital activity and that without the services you provide, the world would probably grind to a halt. Or, maybe you're not a bookkeeper at all, but the owner of a small business skim-reading these pages as fast as possible. You want to get your books done with a minimum of fuss, and maximum speed. You hate messing around with receipts, despise filing and feel ill at the very thought of tax returns. That's okay! In the end, the 'work' of bookkeeping actually works for you.

Think of bookkeeping as a means to an end. Whatever your dreams, whether they're to own your home outright, put the family business back on its feet or sail around the world in a 30-foot yacht, nothing much is going to happen if you don't keep good tabs on your finances. And guess what? You can't keep tabs on your finances unless you do your books.

Quit counting sheep

Am I preaching to the converted with all this chat about the importance of bookkeeping? Maybe you're someone who knows what it means to lie awake at night counting sheep, worrying that the sheep don't balance.

To you, I have a slightly different message. In this book, I encourage you to cast away your magnifying glass and grab a telescope instead. Sure, you've mastered the fine detail, but now you're ready to move ahead and start looking at financial statements. Is the business making a profit? How does this year compare to last year? Is the business growing at a steady rate?

Surprisingly, I find a lot of bookkeepers don't give a second thought to financial reports. Even business owners sometimes get so preoccupied generating sales and paying bills that the only measure of profitability becomes how much is left in the bank account.

Don't miss out on the fun. As a bookkeeper, spend the time to read through Profit & Loss reports and Balance Sheets. You can help the owner understand what's going on in their business, and chances are when you read these reports, you can spot any mistakes you've made. As a business owner, these financial reports are the reward for all your hard bookkeeping efforts.

Want to know more? Feel welcome to skip ahead to Chapter 9, which gives the low-down on both Balance Sheets and Profit & Loss reports.

Do your job well

Whether you're a professional bookkeeper or a business owner, you almost certainly want to get this bookkeeping lark over with as swiftly as possible. The stumbling block is figuring out how not to overcomplicate things. I'm often taken aback at how much time people take to do their books, wasting hours checking and double-checking, shuffling paper from one place to another.

I'm not suggesting compromising quality in order to get a job done quickly, but I am suggesting you put efficient systems in place, right from the word 'go'. As you read this book, I give you my hard-won advice on the best way to approach a task. As you read, ask yourself: 'Am I doing this task in the most efficient way?' 'Can I streamline processes by taking advantage of new technology?' and 'How can I avoid entering things twice?'

Getting Skilled Up

I often get asked by business owners 'Do I need to do a bookkeeping course?' For most small business owners, I reply that no, a course isn't necessary. You may need help from your accountant, or some guidance from handy references like this one or the more in-depth version of this title (called *Bookkeeping For Dummies*, and written by yours truly). However, with a bit of patience, you should be able to master the basics without having to get any formal qualifications. (I devote a lot of space to explaining everyday bookkeeping tasks in chapters 6, 7 and 8.)

However, if you intend on working as a contract bookkeeper, providing bookkeeping services to lots of different businesses, then you almost certainly need formal qualifications in order to meet the stringent regulations that came into effect in 2010.

Working as a contract bookkeeper

If you have your own bookkeeping business, or you're thinking about starting your own bookkeeping business, you must first make sure you have all the necessary bits of paper.

The new BAS agent laws came into effect on 1 March, 2010, along with the introduction of a national Tax Practitioners Board. Only bookkeepers who register with the board — and have the qualifications to do so — are able to provide 'BAS services' for their clients.

A Business Activity Statement (BAS) is a report that all businesses that are registered for GST must complete either monthly or quarterly, summarising how much GST and other taxes are owing.

To put it simply, the laws that govern providing BAS services work like this:

- ✔ You have to register as a BAS agent if clients rely on your expertise *and* you assist clients with 'BAS services'. The definition of BAS services is very broad, and doesn't just mean completing Business Activity Statements, but includes anything to do with GST or PAYG, including configuring tax codes in accounting software, coding tax invoices or generating employee payment summaries.

- ✔ You don't have to register as a BAS agent if you're an employee receiving wages *or* you only do basic bookkeeping data entry based on explicit instructions provided by the client or by their tax agent.

In other words, relatively few contract bookkeepers in Australia aren't caught by this legislation.

If you're not registered as a BAS agent, don't even think about providing any kind of tax advice to a client. The penalty for providing BAS services without registering ranges from a not insignificant $5,500 to a whopping $137,500 per offence.

Registering as a BAS agent

Sadly, registering as a BAS agent isn't quite as simple as signing up for karaoke night at the bar or getting a new Facebook account. Before you can register, you have to make the grade as far as the Tax Practitioners Board is concerned.

Asides from the rather pompously expressed requirement that you're a 'fit and proper person' — that you're not an undischarged bankrupt, you've never served time in jail, been convicted of fraud, tax or otherwise — the main hurdle is the education requirements.

If you have a qualification equivalent to or better than Certificate IV Financial Services (Accounting) or Certificate IV Financial Services (Bookkeeping) *and* you've successfully completed a course in basic GST and BAS principles approved by the board *and* you've undertaken at least 1,400 hours of relevant experience in the preceding three years, then you're home and hosed. You can apply to become a BAS agent before the night is out.

Alternatively, you can apply to become a BAS agent if you're a member of a 'Recognised Professional Association' (which currently includes the ACCA, ATMA, CIMA, CPA, ICAA, NIA and TIA) *and* you've successfully completed a course in basic GST and BAS principles approved by the board *and* you have at least 1,000 hours of relevant experience in the last three years.

For the latest information on registration requirements, check out the BAS agent page at the Tax Practitioners Board website (www.tpb.gov.au) or the BAS agent page at the Institute of Certified Bookkeepers (ICB) website (www.icb.org.au).

Signing up to a course

Professional bookkeeping associations such as AAT Australia and the Institute of Certified Bookkeepers recommend that professional bookkeepers gain a minimum qualification of Certificate IV Financial Services (Accounting) or Certificate IV Financial Services (Bookkeeping). Other possible bookkeeping qualifications include a Diploma of Accounting or an Advanced Diploma of Accounting.

If you're not sure whether you're ready to commit to formal bookkeeping qualifications, you could try one of the more general bookkeeping courses offered by community colleges or private training organisations. Bear in mind that if you do a course that isn't run by a nationally recognised Registered Training Organisation, you may not receive credits if you decide to go on to more formal study, and that this study won't count towards registration as a BAS agent.

The other training that could work for you is to do a one-day or two-day course specific to whatever accounting software you're using, such as an MYOB or QuickBooks course. These courses are good at getting you started with doing the books for your business, but you won't get the same kind of theoretical understanding about how bookkeeping works as you would with a more specific bookkeeping course. You also won't receive any kind of formal qualification.

Chapter 2

Creating a Framework

. . . .

In This Chapter

▶ Finding a home for every single transaction

▶ Gathering materials with account classifications

▶ Building foundations for your Profit & Loss report

▶ Making everything just right with Balance Sheet accounts

▶ Producing your first chart of accounts

. . . .

*I*f bookkeeping were just about doing your tax, the way you categorise information would be pretty simple. Income would be just one total, and most expenses would be lumped together, with only stuff like bank interest, rent and wages separated on reports.

However, your job as a bookkeeper is about much more than tax. You want to generate reports that explain exactly where your income comes from, which activities generate the most moolah, what the expenses are, how actual results compare against budgets, and lots more.

The way you categorise business transactions — in other words, the names of the accounts you use — provides the key to generating this kind of clued-up business reporting. Figuring out the accounts required takes a few smarts, because every business is unique and needs a custom-made list of accounts. But when complete, this list forms the framework for every business report.

In this chapter, I help you to build your own list of accounts. I wax lyrical about the differences between an asset and a liability, between income and expenses, and between earthlings and aliens. Discover how to set up a killer list of accounts that not only keeps the tax bigwigs happy, but helps this business flourish to boot.

Putting Everything in Its Place

When I first worked as a bookkeeper, in the dim and distant past (but *not* before the dinosaurs, as my children claim), I worked with traditional handwritten ledgers. The cash disbursements ledger looked a little like Figure 2-1, with dates and amounts listed down the left-hand side, and a series of columns all the way across, with a different column for each kind of expense.

Regardless of how you do your books these days, the concept remains the same. If you work with handwritten books or even a spreadsheet, chances are that your books look pretty similar to Figure 2-1. Even with accounting software, the core information remains constant. Figure 2-2 shows the same transactions in QuickBooks, with a column for the date, the cheque number, a description, the allocation account and the amount.

Date	Number	Payee	Amount	Cost of Goods Sold	Bank Charges	Electricity	Motor Vehicle	Super	Telephone	Wages
1/06/10	eft	Pinchy Pty Ltd	$ 925.00				$925.00			
1/06/10	1023	China Clothing Imports	$ 325.00	$ 325.00						
2/06/10	eft	Andrew Averly	$ 680.00							$680.00
2/06/10	1024	Rajah Furniture	$ 1,825.00	$ 1,825.00						
5/06/10	eft	ANZ	$ 15.00		$15.00					
5/06/10	eft	Optical Phone Networks	$ 456.00						$ 456.00	
5/06/10	eft	Manchester Unitity Super	$ 920.00					$920.00		
			$ 5,146.00	$ 2,150.00	$15.00	$ -	$925.00	$920.00	$ 456.00	$680.00

Figure 2-1: A handwritten cash disbursements ledger.

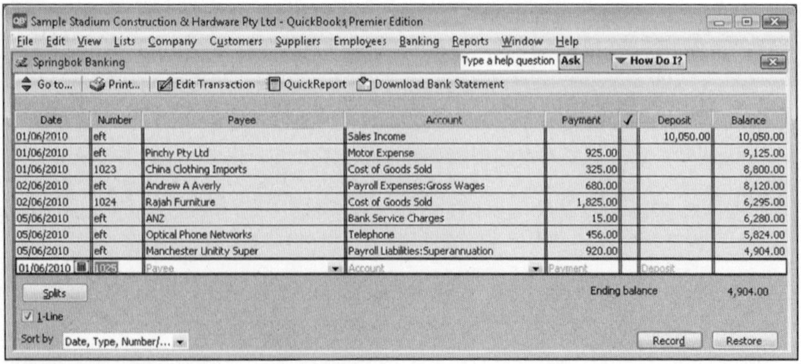

Figure 2-2: A bank register in QuickBooks.

In both Figure 2-1 and Figure 2-2, the choice of account is crucial. In Figure 2-1, the accounts are the headings that run along the top of each column. In Figure 2-2, the account appears in the bank register next to the name of the person being paid.

Your job, as Bookkeeper-Chief-in-Command, is to decide exactly what these accounts should be. (After all, how can you record transactions if you don't know where to put 'em?) The rest of this chapter gives lots of tips about how.

Classifying Accounts

A *chart of accounts* is the list of accounts to which you allocate transactions. These accounts describe what a business owns and what it owes, where money comes from and where money goes.

Accounts fall into six broad classifications:

- ✔ **Assets:** Things owned by the business, such as cash, money in bank accounts, computers, buildings, motor vehicles and so on.

- ✔ **Liabilities:** The stuff that keeps people up at night, such as credit card debts, supplier accounts, tax owing and bank loans.

- ✔ **Equity:** The owner's stake in the business, made up of money invested initially, or accumulated profit/loss built up over time.

- ✔ **Income:** Income, quite simply, is money generated from sales to customers or returns on investments.

- ✔ **Cost of sales:** What it costs in raw materials, supplies or production labour to make the goods that you sell.

- ✔ **Expenses:** Business overheads, such as advertising, bank charges, interest expense, rent or wages.

Assets, liabilities and equity belong in the Balance Sheet. Income, cost of sales and expenses belong in the Profit & Loss. Knowing where transactions end up helps you to classify everything correctly, and with this in hand, creating financial statements is easy as pie.

I explore each of these account classifications in much more detail later in this chapter, discussing what kinds of accounts typically belong under each one.

Setting Up Your Profit & Loss Accounts

How you build your Profit & Loss accounts depends on what kind of system you're using. If you're working with handwritten books or a spreadsheet, then the accounts are simply the headings of the columns where you list transactions. If you're working with accounting software, you typically go to either your Accounts List (in MYOB) or your Chart of Accounts (in QuickBooks).

When I'm helping bookkeepers set up accounts for a business, I always start by making sure these accounts make sense. I don't hesitate to add or delete accounts, change account names or re-organise the order of accounts. This way, I'm sure my clients end up with information that provides the maximum punch for the minimum pain. (Now I come to think of it, that maximum punch/minimum pain scenario sounds depressingly like my son's high school study tactics.)

Analysing income streams

Most businesses have more than one stream of income. Maybe you're a builder who earns money from new houses, as well as renovations and extensions. Maybe you're like me and earn money from a combination of journalism, consulting and teaching. Or maybe you're a musician who also does a bit of teaching on the side.

As a bookkeeper, think about the different sources of income a business generates. If you have fewer than five income accounts, have a think about how you could describe your income in more detail. Each major source of income needs a separate income account. For example, my friend who is a builder divides income into four accounts: Bathroom Sales, Kitchen Sales, Tile Sales and Renovations. This way, he generates regular Profit & Loss reports that reflect how his business generates revenue.

Accountants also like to talk about *other income* or *abnormal income*. Other income or abnormal income includes any income that's not really part of your everyday business, such as interest income, one-off capital gains or gifts from mysterious great-aunties. Other income gets reported separately at the bottom of a Profit & Loss report.

Separating cost of sales accounts

Whatever kind of business you have, you probably have
some expenses that directly relate to sales. In accounting
jargon, expenses that directly relate to sales are called
variable expenses. Expenses that don't directly relate to sales
are called *fixed expenses* or *overheads*.

Variable expenses are classified as *cost of sales accounts*. The
idea is that when sales go up, cost of sales goes up, and when
sales go down, cost of sales goes down. My consumption
of chocolate brownies and my waistline function in just the
same way.

The kind of expenses that you categorise as cost of sales
accounts depend on the nature of the business concerned. Here
are a few examples to help you figure out what's what:

- ✔ **Manufacturing company:** Cost of sales accounts include
  raw materials, electricity, production labour and factory
  rental.

- ✔ **Real estate agent:** Cost of sales accounts include
  advertising, agent commissions and signage.

- ✔ **Retailer:** Retailers usually have a single cost of sales
  account simply called Purchases. Here's where you allocate
  any stuff you buy for reselling to customers.

- ✔ **Tradesperson:** Cost of sales accounts include materials,
  equipment hire and subcontract labour.

Confused? If you're unsure whether an account is a cost of sales
account or an expense account, ask yourself this question:
Does this expense immediately increase if sales increase? If so,
chances are this expense is a cost of sales account.

Cataloguing expenses

Expenses are the day-to-day running costs of your business and
include things like advertising, bank fees and charges, computer
consumables, electricity, motor vehicle, rent, telephone and
administration wages. Accountants also sometimes refer to
expenses as *overheads*.

As a bookkeeper, make sure you tailor the expense accounts to the business concerned. On one hand, you don't want to create too many accounts (I once saw a chart of accounts where there was a different expense account for every employee, and with over 25 employees this became ridiculous). On the other hand, if a business has a particular expense that makes up a large proportion of its expenditure, additional analysis can help.

Here are some expenses I usually include in a list of accounts:

✔ **Accounting Fees:** I keep accounting fees separate from contract bookkeeping fees, so I can easily monitor what each service costs a business.

✔ **Bank Fees:** Use this account for the regular transaction fees you get on your bank account. If you get charged merchant fees — which you will do if customers pay by credit card — you need a separate account for merchant fees.

✔ **Computer Expense:** I dump expenses for stuff like CDs, incidental software and printer ink into this account. I also often create additional expense accounts for Internet Expense and/or Website Maintenance.

✔ **Dues & Subscriptions:** Here's the spot for licence fees, professional memberships, magazine subscriptions and similar items.

✔ **Electricity & Gas:** This is where you can catalogue your personal contribution to climate change.

✔ **Home Office Expense:** If a business operates from home, you may include expenses such as electricity, mortgage interest, rates and repairs in this account. (However, check with the accountant first regarding what home office expenses can be claimed.)

✔ **Insurance:** If you have hefty insurance bills, I suggest you create a header account called Insurance Expense and, underneath, create detail or subaccounts for different kinds of insurance, such as Building and Contents Insurance or Public Liability Insurance.

I usually tuck the insurance for vehicles under the Motor Vehicles header, rather than the Insurance header, because when you report for tax, you need to report separately for motor vehicle expenses.

✔ **Interest Expense:** Don't get muddled between bank charges and interest. Bank statements always differentiate clearly between the two; all you have to do is be alert to the difference.

✔ **Motor Vehicle Expense:** Again, maybe make a header account called Motor Vehicle Expense and, underneath, create subaccounts for fuel, maintenance, registration and so on.

✔ **Office Expense:** You can use this account for squillions of different things, from printing and stationery to paper and pens, from a new office chair to a new filing cabinet. Just make sure you're clear about the distinction between an expense and an asset.

✔ **Rent Expense:** Unless you work out of a home office, you almost certainly pay rent on an office or factory.

✔ **Salaries & Wages:** If you have more than a handful of employees, consider creating detail accounts or subaccounts for the different categories of employees (see the sidebar 'Under the microscope' later in the chapter). For example, a restaurant may have three accounts; one account for kitchen staff, another for front-of-house staff and another for management.

✔ **Superannuation:** I suggest you create two superannuation expense accounts: one for employees and one for directors or business owners.

✔ **Telephone:** If telephone expenses are high, create two accounts: one for office phone and the other for mobile phone.

✔ **Travel & Entertainment:** If you travel overseas, remember to separate domestic and overseas travel. And if you spend money on entertainment, remember to trawl through the many thousands of pages of legislation to see what's deductible and what's not. (In fact, the legislation is so complex you're probably best to speak to your accountant for advice.)

By the way, accountants sometimes also use *other expenses* as an additional account classification. Other expenses are abnormal expenses that aren't part of your everyday business, such as lawsuit expenses, capital losses or entertaining aliens from outer space.

Under the microscope

If you're working with accounting software, a good way to get your accounts really organised is to use headers. For example, if you create a header account and name it Motor Vehicle Expenses, you can then add many accounts below this heading, such as Fuel Expense, Registration and Repairs & Maintenance.

The terminology when grouping accounts in MYOB software is *header accounts* and *detail accounts* and, in QuickBooks, *header accounts* and *subaccounts*. Header accounts are the headings (surprisingly enough) and appear in bold in the list of accounts. Detail or subaccounts are the accounts that belong under each header.

When designing a chart of accounts, I recommend you identify any areas of major expense and try to categorise these expenses into a bit more detail. For example, one of my clients spends up big on advertising. I created five different accounts to analyse his advertising expenditure, separating newsletter mail-outs, trade stands, sponsored listings, print media and public relations. My client likes the additional analysis these detail accounts provide, and the bookkeeper finds the system quite easy to manage.

Itemising Balance Sheet Accounts

If a business is already up and running, and has already completed the first year of business, an easy way to see what Balance Sheet accounts are required is to get your hands on last year's Balance Sheet report from the accountant.

If a business is new, you can simply create new Balance Sheet accounts as and when you need them. However, read through the next few pages to get an idea of what accounts you may need to get you started.

Adding up the assets (ah, joy of joys)

So what's an asset? Is it your pearly white teeth, your fine singing voice or your generous nature? None of these things, I'm afraid. The International Accounting Standards Board defines an *asset* as 'a resource controlled by the enterprise as a result of past events and from which future economic benefits are expected to flow to the enterprise'.

Hmmm. My mind goes to mush when faced with this kind of talk, so I'm going to put it more simply: Assets are the good stuff, including anything you own, such as computers, office equipment, motor vehicles and cash.

Accountants like to classify assets according to how readily these assets can be converted into cash, typically using the headings *current assets*, *non-current assets* (also called *fixed assets*) and *intangible assets*.

Current assets

A *current asset* is anything that a business owns that can realistically be converted into cash within the next 12 months.

The kinds of things that get lumped into current assets include

- **Bank accounts and cash:** Accounts that fall into this account type include petty cash, cheque accounts, savings accounts, term deposits and so on.

- **Short-term investments:** No, I'm not talking about your latest love. I'm thinking of nerdy stuff such as shares or unit trust holdings.

- **Accounts receivable:** *Accounts receivable* is the bookkeeping term for money that customers owe you. (Accountants sometimes refer to this account as *trade debtors*.)

- **Inventory:** Another old-fashioned bookkeeping term, *inventory* is the word bookkeepers use for stock or raw materials that get sold to customers or assembled to make goods.

- **Prepayments:** Smaller businesses don't usually account for prepayments, but larger businesses make adjustments for things such as prepaid insurance, rent in advance or deposits paid to suppliers.

- **Work in progress:** Work in progress includes jobs that have started but aren't yet complete.

Non-current assets

This classification (also sometimes known as *fixed assets*) is for anything physical that you can touch, feel and see, but that isn't readily converted to cash. Sounds kind of sensual but I'm talking about relatively mundane things such as office equipment, land and buildings, computers and motor vehicles.

- **Land and buildings:** So if a business buys a block of land or a building, this is the account to choose.

- **Plant and equipment:** Completely unrelated to potting mix, this rather agricultural sounding account includes stuff like new computers, telephone systems, machinery and tools.

- **Motor vehicles:** Yep, that banged up rusty old heap is actually an asset, not a liability.

- **Accumulated depreciation:** Yet another weird expression, meaning the amount the accountant has already claimed back on assets.

Intangible assets

An *intangible asset* is something that is worth something, but that you can't touch, smell or see. Intangible assets are usually not readily convertible into cash. (My husband assures me that his sense of humour is one of his intangible assets. At times, however, I reckon it's more of a liability.)

Three of the most common intangible assets are borrowing expenses, formation expenses and goodwill.

- **Borrowing expenses:** For example, if you were to take out a $50,000 loan over five years, and the bank charged a one-off fee of $1,000, the accountant may choose to allocate this expense to an asset account called Borrowing Expenses and amortise this expense over the period of the loan.

- **Formation expenses:** Formation expenses usually relate to the cost of setting up a company. Because formation expenses aren't tax-deductible, some accountants choose to show these expenses as an asset. (Other accountants write off formation expenses straightaway, and make a tax adjustment in the final return.)

    ✔ **Goodwill:** Goodwill is another example of an intangible
asset. Many businesses don't put a value on goodwill
until they sell the business to someone else. At that point,
goodwill becomes part of the purchase price and shows up
on the Balance Sheet as an intangible asset.

Listing liabilities (oh, woe is me)

Liabilities are the stuff that keeps you awake at night. You
know, bulging credit card accounts, supplier bills, GST owing,
hideous bank loans and that unmentionable loan from your
parents-in-law.

In the same way as accountants like to bundle assets into
groups, they do the same with liabilities.

Current liabilities

A *current liability* is an amount owed by the business which is
due within a one-year period. The kinds of accounts that sit
under current liabilities include

    ✔ **Credit cards:** I recommend bookkeepers think of credit
cards in the same way as any other bank account. It's just
that the business owes the bank money, rather than the
other way around. Strangely enough, simply ignoring credit
card bills and pretending they don't exist doesn't seem to
work as a strategy.

    ✔ **Overdrafts:** Again, you treat an overdraft in the same way
as a regular bank account.

    ✔ **Accounts payable:** *Accounts payable* (also called *trade
creditors*) is the term for money that you owe to suppliers.

    ✔ **Other current liabilities:** This category covers any other
liabilities that are relatively short term, such as customer
deposits, employee wages, tax owing, GST owing or short-
term director loans.

Non-current liabilities

A *non-current liability* is anything you owe that isn't due to be
paid out within the next 12 months. The kinds of accounts that
sit under non-current liabilities include

    ✔ **Hire purchase debts:** Hire purchase debts are usually non-
current liabilities because they're payable over several
years (although some accountants prefer to split hire

purchase debts into current and non-current liabilities). Hire purchase liability accounts come complete with a partner, a strange account that goes by the name 'Unexpired Interest Charges' or 'Future HP Interest Charges'.

✔ **Bank loans or mortgages:** You know what these are. Seems that banks are always in on the act.

Accounting for equity

Equity is a fancy term for the 'interest' that a director or an owner has in the business, including both capital contributed and the profit or loss built up over time. The kind of equity accounts you need when bookkeeping depend on whether the business has a sole trader, partnership or company structure.

Out on your own (sole trader accounts)

Sole trader equity accounts include Owner's Capital, Current Year's Profits and Owner's Drawings. As a bookkeeper, the only equity accounts you allocate transactions to are Owner's Drawings, which is the account where you allocate any personal spending by the owner, and Owner's Contributions, where you allocate personal contributions from the owner.

Sometimes, if a small business owner has only one bank account and uses this account for both business and personal spending, I create several Owner's Drawings accounts. For example, a client of mine has one account called 'Owner's Drawings Mortgage Payments', another account called 'Owner's Drawings Tax Payments' and another account called 'All Other Owner's Drawings'.

Takes two to tango (partnerships)

With a partnership, each partner has both a Partner's Capital account and a Partner's Drawings account. At the end of each year, the accountant also uses a Distribution of Profit account for each partner. (The Partner Capital accounts, when added together, are equivalent to Retained Earnings in a company.)

As a bookkeeper, the only accounts you use on a regular basis are the Partner's Drawings accounts.

Although partnerships don't require an account called Retained Earnings, if you're working with accounting software, you usually find this account is a default account that you can't delete (at the end of each financial year, current year's earnings 'roll over' into this Retained Earnings account). You can rename this account to become one of the Partner's Capital accounts. The accountant can then provide a journal at the end of each year that adjusts the partnership capital accounts.

Aiming high (companies and trusts)

Companies typically have Retained Earnings, Current Year's Earnings, Dividends Paid and Shareholder Capital as the equity accounts. Occasionally, companies also have reserve accounts, such as an Asset Revaluation Reserve.

Retained earnings are the income that a company holds onto, and doesn't distribute to shareholders. Retained earnings (or losses) are cumulative, building up from one year to the next. When shareholders receive a profit distribution, you allocate this payment to an equity account called Dividends Paid.

Trusts have a similar equity account structure to companies, but have an account called Issued Ordinary Units or Trust Equity instead of Share Capital. When trust beneficiaries receive a profit distribution, you allocate this payment to an equity account called Trust Distributions Paid.

Don't allocate any transactions to equity accounts for a company or for a trust unless instructed to do so by an accountant.

You may be wondering where to allocate personal spending by company directors. Either allocate personal spending to Directors' Wages (in which case you need to allow for wages and superannuation), or allocate personal spending to a liability account called Directors' Loan.

Building a Final Chart of Accounts

In Figure 2-3, you can see some of the accounts that make up the final chart of accounts for a wholesale business. The format of this chart of accounts is typical (listing account name, type, balance and so on), but remember that just as every business is unique, so every chart of accounts is unique also.

Accounts List

	All Accounts	Asset	Liability	Equity	Income	Cost of Sales	Expense	Other Income	Other Expense

	Account Name	Type	Tax	Linked	Balance
⇨	3-9000 Current Year Earnings	Equity	N-T	✓	$835,446.28
⇨	3-9999 Historical Balancing	Equity	N-T	✓	$0.00
⇨	4-0000 Income	Income			$1,538,824.92
⇨	4-1000 Sales - Item A	Income	GST		$1,146,738.00
⇨	4-1300 Sales - Item B	Income	GST		$389,570.00
⇨	4-3000 Interest Received	Income	FRE		$250.78
⇨	4-4000 Freight Charged to Customers	Income	GST	✓	$846.10
⇨	4-9999 Currency Gain Loss	Income	N-T	✓	$1,420.04
⇨	5-0000 Cost Of Sales	Cost of Sales			$692,388.57
⇨	5-1000 Purchase of Stock	Cost of Sales	GST	✓	$672,873.38
⇨	5-2000 Packaging	Cost of Sales	GST	✓	$6,188.09
⇨	5-3000 Shipping Charges	Cost of Sales	GST		$13,327.10
⇨	6-0000 Expenses	Expense			$10,990.07
⇨	6-1100 Accountancy Fees	Expense	GST		$377.00
⇨	6-1600 Bank Charges	Expense	FRE		$1,270.78
⇨	6-2100 Computer Consumables	Expense	GST		$6,291.17
⇨	6-2200 Depreciation	Expense	N-T		$0.00
⇨	6-2300 Dues & Subscriptions	Expense	GST		$0.00
⇨	6-2850 Electricity & Gas Expense	Expense	GST		$41.60
⇨	6-2920 Insurance Expense	Expense	GST		$0.00
⇨	6-5500 Legal Costs	Expense	GST		$2,642.52
⇨	6-5600 Motor Vehicle Expenses	Expense	GST		$367.00
⇨	6-8000 Salaries	Expense			$0.00
⇨	6-8100 Wages & Salaries	Expense	N-T	✓	$0.00
⇨	6-8300 Superannuation Expense	Expense	N-T	✓	$0.00
⇨	8-0000 Other Income	Other Income			$0.00
⇨	8-1000 Gain on Sale of Assets	Other Income	N-T		$0.00
⇨	9-0000 Other Expenses	Other Expense			$0.00

📤 Up   📥 Down   🗐 Combine Accounts

? Help F1   Print   New   Budgets   Edit   Close

Figure 2-3: A final chart of accounts, ready for action.

One feature with accounting software is that you usually get a choice of a few dozen templates when getting started. You can pick your business type from this list of templates and with three clicks of your heels have a complete chart of accounts ready to go. However, although a standard template seems like a quick way to get started, you may end up wasting hours customising this accounts list to suit. If the standard template isn't a good fit, you're best to start from scratch building your own chart of accounts.

Painting by numbers

By now, you probably get a sense of how crucial account classifications are to bookkeeping (whether something is an income or expense, an asset or liability).

In MYOB, account classifications are clearly identified. All assets start with the number 1, liabilities with the number 2, equity accounts with the number 3, income accounts with the number 4, cost of sales accounts with the number 5 and expense accounts with the number 6.

Within each account classification you also get account types, so that if something is an asset for example, you choose whether this asset is a bank account, an accounts receivable account, a fixed asset or another kind of asset.

In QuickBooks, most bookkeepers choose not to use account numbering, and rely on names instead. However, the account types are still clearly defined, with five different account types for both assets and liabilities.

Chapter 3

Going for the Big Equation

*I*f you want to be a racing driver, it pays to understand something about the mechanics of a car. If all you want to do is drive from A to B, then you can rely on others to bail you out, and go from one year to the next without looking under the bonnet.

The same goes for bookkeeping. If you're a business owner and you want to do your books in a simple fashion, giving them to your accountant for the finishing touches, then you can get by without ever worrying about double-entry bookkeeping. (Yep, you're off the hook — you can skip reading this chapter and proceed to the more interesting stuff.)

However, if you're serious about bookkeeping, knowing the theory of how bookkeeping works and what goes on behind the scenes is vital. An understanding of debits and credits — which form the bones of double-entry bookkeeping — is essential for many of the more skilled activities a bookkeeper undertakes, such as adjusting accounts via journal entries, making sense of a Balance Sheet or troubleshooting account balances.

In this chapter, I explore all the ins and outs of double-entry bookkeeping, and how to figure out debits and credits for most everyday transactions. I also talk about the difference between cash and accrual accounting, and how to choose which system is going to work best for you.

Matchmaking with Debits and Credits

Way back in the distant mists of time, over 500 years ago, an Italian mathematician by the name of Pacioli wrote a rave about bookkeeping, culminating in a brilliant equation that falls only one step short of Einstein's theory of relativity. The equation goes:

Assets = Liabilities + Owner's Equity

Pacioli expanded on this formula by articulating that all asset, cost of sales and expense accounts are debit balances, and all liability, equity and income accounts are credit balances. This leads to Paco's second equation:

Debits = Credits

Pacioli's idea was that for every financial transaction that takes place, there's both a debit and a credit. Just like yin and yang, man and woman, property developer and politician.

Sounds a little bizarre, right? Read on to put theory into practice.

Studying a little give and take

So, every transaction in accounting is either a *debit* or a *credit*. A debit is any transaction that increases assets or expenses, or that decreases liabilities, equity or income. A credit is any transaction that increases liabilities, equity or income, or that decreases assets or expenses.

Table 3-1 provides a summary of debits and credits in action.

Table 3-1	Debits and Credits in Action	
Account Type	*To Increase This Account*	*To Decrease This Account*
Asset	Debit	Credit
Liability	Credit	Debit
Equity	Credit	Debit
Income	Credit	Debit
Expenses	Debit	Credit

Bookkeeping journals generally have five columns and at least three separate lines per transaction: On the first line you write the date, reference number and account name being debited, plus an amount in the debit column on the left; on the second line you write the account being credited, plus an amount in the credit column on the right; and on the third line you write a short memo describing the journal. Figure 3-1 shows how this works. (*Note:* This example is simplified for the purposes of my example, and doesn't include GST.)

Date	Reference	Account	Debit	Credit
30/09/2010	GJ001	Motor Vehicles at Cost	$ 15,000.00	
		Bank Loan		$ 15,000.00
		Purchase of new motor vehicle		
30/09/2010	GJ002	Grants Received in Advance	$ 2,500.00	
		Grant Income		$ 2,500.00
		Journalling of grant money received last year, paid in advance		

Figure 3-1: A journal entry includes a column for debits and a column for credits.

This journal may look peculiar, but the concepts to remember are as follows:

- ✔ The debits column is on the left, and credits on the right.

- ✔ Whenever you allocate an entry to an asset account that increases the balance of this account, you put the amount in the debit column. (This means, incidentally, that if you increase your bank account, this is a debit, not a credit. Weird, heh?)

- ✔ Whenever you allocate an entry to a liability account that increases the balance of this account, you put the amount in the credit column.

- ✔ When you pay out an expense, the expense goes in the debit column.

- ✔ When you receive money, the income goes in the credit column.

Lynley's cheats' guide to debits and credits

Lynley (who wrote the New Zealand content for *Bookkeeping For Dummies,* Australian & New Zealand Edition), offers a handy acronym handed down from Don Little, her old accounting tutor at Auckland College of Education. Don's words were 'never teach this to your students', a warning that only served as encouragement for Lynley to teach this rule to literally hundreds of students over the last 20 years. Here's the acronym:

DEAD CLIC

This acronym stands for **D**ebit **E**xpenses, **A**ssets and **D**rawings, and **C**redit **L**iabilities, **I**ncome and **C**apital. You apply this DEAD CLIC rule if an account goes up in value. If an account goes down in value, you apply the opposite. In other words, if an expense increases in value, then you debit the account (because the DEAD CLIC rule says to **D**ebit **E**xpenses). If an expense decreases in value, then you credit the account.

Makes this whole debits and credits lark easy to remember, don't you reckon?

Following a modern fable

Debits and credits in accounting are strange to get your head around, but an example helps to bring these weird principles to life. Say Jamie receives $5 from his mum to buy some lemonade. Jamie, being just a tad on the nerdy side, asks himself, what are those rules again?

Assets = Liabilities + Owner's Equity

and

Debits = Credits

Jamie muses for a while and applies this rule to his business venture so far. He has assets of five bucks, so he debits his cash account. And his stake in the business is the same amount, so he credits his equity account.

**Assets in cash $5 = Liabilities (none) + Equity
(capital contributions) $5**

Jamie then scrounges $2 from his dad. Dad is grumpy and says this is a loan only. Applying his accounting principles, Jamie debits his cash account and credits his liability account. He now has

**Assets in cash $7 = Liability $2 + Equity
(capital contributions) $5**

Jamie then plays truant from school and buys seven bottles of lemonade for $1 each. He runs off to the protest march in town, where he sells each bottle at $1.50. With this transaction, he increases his cash (a debit), and increases income (a credit). He returns home with $10.50 in his pocket, having made a profit of $3.50. Jamie now has

**Assets in cash $10.50 = Liability $2 + Equity $8.50
(capital of $5 and current earnings of $3.50)**

At this point, Jamie's Profit & Loss report shows income of $10.50, cost of sales of $7 and a profit of $3.50. Note that the profit at the bottom of the Profit & Loss report is the same figure as current earnings in the Balance Sheet.

So there you have it: An explanation of debits and credits and why a Balance Sheet always balances.

Putting Theory into Practice

In this section, I explain how to put debits and credits into practice using everyday transactions such as sales, customer payments and supplier payments.

Here's my fail-safe method (ignoring GST):

1. **Decide what accounts are involved.**

   Don't forget you often get more than two accounts in a single transaction, especially if GST is involved.

2. **For each account involved in this transaction, decide what kind of account it is.**

   Are the accounts assets or liabilities, income or expenses? If you're not sure, refer back to Chapter 2 for an explanation of every account type.

3. **Decide whether the balance of these accounts is increasing or decreasing.**

   For example, if you pay money out of your bank account, the balance of your bank account goes down, and the balance of whatever expense account is affected goes up.

4. **Figure out whether you need to debit or credit each account in order for your transaction to make sense.**

   Table 3-1 to the rescue. For example, to decrease the balance of your bank account, you need a credit, and to increase the balance of an expense account, you need a debit.

5. **Record your transaction.**

   Earlier in this chapter, Figure 3-1 shows a typical journal entry, with information about the accounts that you're debiting and crediting, as well as a date and a reference number.

6. **Check your work.**

   If a journal entry affects a bank account, one easy way to check your work is to make sure your bank account reconciles (for more about bank reconciliations, see Chapter 8).

Clear as mud? Read on to see how I apply my fail-safe method to several different kinds of transactions.

Moving funds in bank accounts

A friend asked me the other week 'What's the definition of an accountant?' 'Tell me', I replied hesitantly. (My friend is actually married to an accountant, a man with a rather lugubrious temperament reminiscent of Eeyore in *Winnie the Pooh*.) 'An accountant', my friend replied in a rather despairing tone, 'is someone who solves a problem you didn't know you had in a way you don't understand.'

To be sure, this whole business of applying debits and credits feels rather counterintuitive at times. For example, if I deposit money into my bank account, I think to myself, 'Cool, my account is in credit now'. But in fact, if I see life from a warped accounting kind of perspective, what I've done is increase the value of an asset. Looking at Table 3-1, if you increase an asset, this action creates a debit. And indeed, accountants consider an increase in your bank account as a debit, and a decrease as a credit. Yep, the complete opposite of what you expect.

To try and clear up any confusion, I'm going to work through a detailed example, imagining that I've just received a loan for $40,000.

1. **What accounts are involved?**

   With this transaction, I end up with $40,000 more in my bank account, but I also end up with a loan for the same amount.

2. **What types of accounts are affected?**

   Easy. My bank account is an asset (well, on a good day it is), and this new bank loan is most definitely a liability. (Just how badly do I need that new ute, I ask myself.)

3. **Is the balance of these accounts increasing or decreasing?**

   My bank account is increasing, and so is the loan account.

4. **Do I need to debit or credit each account in order for this transaction to make sense?**

   Looking at Table 3-1, if an asset increases, that's a debit. If a liability increases, that's a credit. Ah, how sweet. A debit and a credit, like lovers on a moonlit night. You can see my journal entry in Figure 3-2.

Date	Reference	Account	Debit	Credit
30/09/2010	GJ003	Business Cheque Account	$ 40,000.00	
		Bank Loan		$ 40,000.00
		Business loan from bank. 5 year term, fixed interest		

Figure 3-2: Recording a general journal entry for a new loan.

Taking a peek at sales

Okay, I'm going to apply the whole debits and credits method to a sales transaction where I sell goods to a customer on credit and then a few days later, the customer pays.

Using the method from earlier in this chapter (refer to 'Putting Theory into Practice'), here goes:

1. **Decide what accounts are involved.**

   I'll keep things simple and assume no GST is involved. So the two accounts involved are *Accounts Receivable* (the money that customers owe me) and *Income from Sales*.

2. **Decide what type of accounts these are.**

   I could refer to Chapter 2 for help with this one, but I just happen to know that Accounts Receivable is an asset, and Income from Sales, well, income is an income account. (Something has to be easy.)

3. **Decide whether the balance of these accounts is increasing or decreasing.**

   Accounts Receivable is going to increase, because customers are going to owe me more after the sale. Income from Sales is going to increase also, because I'm making a sale.

4. **Figure out whether you need to debit or credit each account in order for your transaction to make sense.**

   Aha. I look at the handy info in Table 3-1, which tells me that if Accounts Receivable (an asset) increases, that's a debit, and if Income from Sales increases, that's a credit. Yeehaa! I've got a debit and a credit, so I know things are going to balance.

5. **Record your journal.**

See the first journal in Figure 3-3 for how this sale appears.

Date	Reference	Account	Debit	Credit
30/09/2010	Invoice 982	Accounts Receivable	$ 980.00	
		Income from Sales		$ 980.00
		Invoice 982 to Phillip Gwynne		
2/10/2010	CR003	Business Cheque Account	$ 980.00	
		Accounts Receivable		$ 980.00
		Payment of Invoice 982		

Figure 3-3: Two journal entries — one showing a sale, the other showing a payment.

Next, imagine I receive the money from this customer. This time, I know that Accounts Receivable and my Business Cheque Account are the two accounts affected. Accounts Receivable is going to decrease (and Table 3-1 tells me that a decrease in an asset is a credit), and the balance of my Business Cheque Account is going to increase (and I can see that an increase in an asset is a debit). The second journal in Figure 3-3 shows this payment in action.

Checking out expenses

Okay, so what are the journal entries behind an expense payment, such as paying a telephone bill?

Using my step-by-step method, figuring out that your Business Cheque Account and your Telephone Expense account are the two accounts involved is easy. Your Business Cheque Account is an asset and the balance of this account is going to decrease. If assets decrease (refer to Table 3-1), this is a credit. Telephone is an expense account and the balance of this account is going to increase. When expenses increase, this is a debit.

Another debit, another credit. Figure 3-4 shows how it works.

Date	Reference	Account	Debit	Credit
30/09/2010	D/Debit	Telephone Expense	$ 330.00	
		Business Cheque Account		$ 330.00
		Payment of office telephone bill		

Figure 3-4: The journal entry behind the payment of a telephone account.

Throwing GST into the mix

So far, I've been keeping my examples pretty simple, because I want to demonstrate the logic of double-entry bookkeeping. However, things do get more complicated when you pop GST into the mix.

From a bookkeeper's perspective, when you add GST to a sale or a purchase, this tax doesn't affect the amount of income or expense. For example, if you make a sale for $90 and you add GST to this sale, then the GST component isn't income, rather this component is tax owing to the government. In Australia, where GST is 10 per cent, the income on this sale is $90, with $9 GST.

In Figure 3-5, I show the transactions from Figures 3-3 and 3-4 one more time, but I include GST on each transaction. When I record a sale, I credit an account called GST Collected. When I record purchases, I debit an account called GST Paid. (I generally keep GST accounts separate, with one account for GST Collected and another for GST Paid. Some accountants prefer to use a single tax account called Tax Payable. Either method works fine.)

Date	Reference	Account	Debit	Credit
30/09/2010	Invoice 982	Accounts Receivable	$ 980.00	
		Income from Sales		$ 890.91
		GST Collected		$ 89.09
		Invoice 982 to Phillip Gwynne.		
30/09/2010	D/Debit	Telephone Expense	$ 300.00	
		GST Paid	$ 30.00	
		Business Cheque Account		$ 330.00
		Payment of office telephone bill		
2/10/2010	CR003	Business Cheque Account	$ 980.00	
		Accounts Receivable		$ 980.00
		Payment of Invoice 982		

Figure 3-5: Journal entries showing GST in sales and purchase transactions.

Choosing between Cash and Accrual

Before you start to do your books, you need to decide whether you're going to do your books on a cash basis or an accrual basis, or a combination of both. (Cash-basis accounting offers a simpler and faster approach to bookkeeping, but accrual accounting offers more accurate management of information.) This choice of accounting method affects the way you record everyday transactions.

By the way, cash-basis accounting, despite a rather dubious ring to its name, is nothing to do with Mafia characters exchanging wads of cash in the dead of night. Rather, cash-basis accounting is a perfectly respectable way to do your books. Why? Read on ...

Keeping things simple with cash

With *cash-basis accounting* you recognise income only when you receive cash from a customer or pay cash to a supplier. For example, if you sell something on credit, you don't record this sale as income at the point you send the customer an invoice. Instead, you record this sale as income when you receive the dough in your hot, sticky hands.

The same principle applies to purchases. You may receive a bill from a supplier and hold onto it for a couple of weeks before paying it. With cash-basis accounting, you don't record this purchase as an expense at the time you receive the bill. Instead, you record this purchase as an expense when you finally part with the cash.

I use cash-basis accounting for my holiday house business. Guests often pay in advance, some pay at the time, other guests even pay after their stay. However, I don't bother creating an invoice for every transaction. For bookkeeping purposes, I simply get my bank statements and whenever I see money going into my account, I record it as income. (I don't even record the name of the person who paid.) In the same way, I don't worry about recording any bills I owe to suppliers. Only when the money goes out of my bank account do I record the expense in my books.

Cash-basis accounting works well for businesses that don't offer credit to customers, and that don't have a lot of money owing to suppliers. Here are some examples where cash-basis accounting works well:

- ✔ A client of mine makes glass bead jewellery that she sells at markets on weekends. Her books are simple: She banks her takings every week and records this as income, and records expenses only when the money leaves her bank account.

- ✔ Another client is a dentist. He has medical software that keeps track of patient accounts, and so for his bookkeeping, he keeps things simple. He records daily banking by referring to his bank statement, allocating the totals to a single income figure, and records payments to suppliers only when bills are paid.

- ✔ A friend of mine is a handyman. He provides handwritten dockets to his customers on the spot as he finishes each job, and he uses copies of these dockets to keep track of which customers have paid and which haven't. For his bookkeeping, he simply works from his bank statements, recording weekly banking totals and allocating them to income. Similarly, he only records supplier bills in his books when he makes the payment.

The ease of cash-basis accounting works well for small businesses getting started. However, if you want to track how much customers owe you, or how much you owe to suppliers, then accrual accounting works better.

Getting more info with accrual

With *accrual accounting*, you recognise income at the time the sale occurs, regardless of when you receive cash from a customer. Similarly, you recognise expenses at the time you receive a bill from a supplier, regardless of when you pay this bill.

If you use accounting software, and you take advantage of the sales or purchases features, then you automatically do your books on an accrual basis. Unless you specifically ask for a cash-basis report, the financial reports in accounting software report income at the time you make a sale, not when you finally receive payment for it. Similarly, reports show expenses at the time you receive goods or services, not when you finally make a payment.

Accrual accounting works well for businesses that offer credit to customers, and that receive credit accounts from suppliers.

Get the difference with GST

Don't get muddled about the difference between *cash-based accounting* and *cash-based reporting for GST*. One system is not necessarily dependent on the other.

If you use accounting software, you can do your books on an accrual basis, but generate a report that shows GST on a cash basis. This works well for many businesses that use their accounting software to record customer sales but only want to cough up the GST to the tax office after customers have paid.

On the other hand, if you do your books on a cash basis, then making adjustments to report for GST on an accrual basis gets pretty fiddly. This scenario is rare, however, as most businesses that choose to report for GST on an accrual basis also choose to use accrual accounting.

Accrual-based bookkeeping is the most accurate from a management accounting perspective because it produces the most accurate Profit & Loss reports. However, accrual-based bookkeeping usually takes longer than cash-based bookkeeping, so as a bookkeeper, you need to be confident that the extra time taken warrants the improved quality of information provided.

Enjoying a half-half measure

Sometimes it makes sense to use cash-basis accounting for sales and accrual accounting for purchases, or vice versa. For example, many businesses use accounting software to record individual customer sales (accrual accounting), but only record supplier bills as they're paid (cash-basis accounting).

With my consulting and writing business, I combine cash and accrual accounting. I use accrual accounting for billing my customers, recording invoices in my accounting software as soon as work is complete, even though my customers may take weeks (or even months!) to pay. I use cash-basis accounting for my suppliers, only recording expenses in my accounting at the point I pay suppliers.

Remember that for tax purposes (as opposed to bookkeeping purposes), you can only use one method or another. For example, although I do my books on a cash basis for my suppliers and on an accrual basis for sales, when I lodge my tax return, I declare both income and expense on a cash basis. To do this, I make a journal entry once a year that adjusts my income to reflect cash received, rather than sales billed. (Skip to the next heading for more about accounting for tax purposes.)

Using one method for your books, and another for income tax

In some situations, it's okay to have a disparity between your bookkeeping method and your tax accounting method. For example, some businesses use cash-basis accounting for everyday bookkeeping, but use accrual accounting for lodging tax returns. That's okay — once a year, the bookkeeper can make a list for the accountant listing all the bills owing to suppliers or money owing from customers. The accountant can then do an adjustment, converting a set of cash-based books to an accrual-based set of books. This scenario is likely for many small businesses.

Part II
Forming a Plan

Glenn Lumsden

'Every year we end up in the same
situation ... one week to get
our books to the accountant.
What we need is an accountant
lazier than us.'

In this part ...

*I*f you're just getting started with a new business, or you're going into a business where you suspect that the systems are a bit outdated or inefficient, then the next two chapters are written just for you.

In Chapter 4, I explore the decision about whether you need accounting software, and if so, how to choose a system that's going to sing, dance and cook your dinner (or, at least, help you determine if someone is cooking the books).

Then in Chapter 5, I take a look at GST. Surely one of life's more exciting topics, don't you think? I find this chapter truly scintillating, but hey, if you don't feel the same way, why not store this book on your bedside table? Those convoluted tax rulings provide the perfect remedy for sleepless nights.

Chapter 4

Doing Business with Accounting Software

*J*ust in case you're wondering, this chapter isn't about how to use accounting software. Using accounting software and understanding how bookkeeping works are so completely intertwined that I try not to separate the two. Instead, I scatter explanations about using accounting software throughout this book, each time in the context of specific bookkeeping tasks.

In this chapter, I try to answer questions such as 'What's so great about accounting software anyway?', 'What software works best?' and 'Are all those promises that sweet software salesperson made going to come true?' (Sadly when it comes to software, there's no such thing as a broken promise; only unfortunate misunderstandings.)

I also focus on how to get your new accounting system up and running, providing three unbeatable tips: Start at the right time of year (I'll tell you when); do tasks logically step-by-step (I provide a list); and last, keep lots of fine dark chocolate close to hand. You'll soon be firing on all four cylinders, speeding along the freeway to bookkeeping success.

What's so Great about Accounting Software Anyway?

In my opinion, accounting software is one of those rare phenomena where a computer genuinely *saves* time, instead of chewing it up. If you have more than 20 or so transactions a month (and the vast majority of businesses do), then it's a no-brainer: Accounting software is a must.

You may feel defensive reading this emphatic declaration of mine, thinking to yourself that your spreadsheet or handwritten ledgers do just fine. I implore you to stick around and read the next couple of pages, while I present the pros and cons of different methods.

Doing books by hand — is it worth it?

I still come across people who do their books by hand, and I'm well acquainted with the arguments put forward to justify this habit. True to my somewhat adversarial nature, I'm going to present these arguments to you, and refute them, one by one:

- ✔ **'I prefer handwritten books because it's easier to look things up.'** Bunkum. When you do books by hand, transactions are sorted by date, and date only. If you do books on a computer, you can search for transactions by name, date, amount, type of expense, cheque number or whatever your heart desires.

- ✔ **'If the computer dies, I won't lose all my work.'** True, but with accounting software, you won't lose all your work if you have effective backups. And with handwritten books, you only have one copy, which makes you much more vulnerable to theft, fire, flood or any other kind of disaster.

- ✔ **'Handwritten books are quicker.'** No, they're not. Typing is usually the same speed or faster than writing by hand, and you get the added bonus that the computer adds up all the columns automatically. (I used to do books by hand and, believe me, it took hours to get everything to balance.)

✔ **'Handwritten books are easier to understand.'** Maybe, just maybe, this is true, but only if all you're doing is listing transactions. However, as soon as you try to generate a trial balance or Profit & Loss report, then handwritten books become as complex as understanding the psychology of the opposite sex.

✔ **'Handwritten books are cheaper.'** I can't argue with that one. However, entry-level accounting software is cheap as chips, starting at about $150. It doesn't take long before you gain back $150, both in terms of lost time gained, and the benefit of having good financial reports on tap.

So, what do you reckon? It's time to hurl that handwritten ledger out of the window, without so much as checking for innocent passers-by below.

Using spreadsheets instead

Many business owners and bookkeepers spurn accounting software and instead wax lyrical about the nifty little spreadsheet that they use to track everything from their weight-loss program to their business finances.

Spreadsheets are one step up from handwritten books, I agree. However, they don't quite cut the mustard:

✔ **Spreadsheets are vulnerable to error:** You only need to get one formula wrong, maybe missing out a row at the top or the bottom when adding up a column, and your totals are wrong also.

✔ **Spreadsheets only do half the job:** Sure, you can whip up a set of books with a spreadsheet, but you can't use a spreadsheet to generate a customer invoice, a purchase order for a supplier, or employee payslips.

✔ **Spreadsheets don't provide financial reports:** When you key transactions into a spreadsheet, it takes just as long as keying transactions into accounting software. But when you're done, all you get is a list of totals. You don't get a Profit & Loss report, a Balance Sheet, a neat report showing how much GST you owe, or any of the other reports that are part and parcel of any accounting software.

In other words, why do something half-baked when you can do it superbly instead?

Choosing the One that's Right for You

'Choosing the One that's Right for You' makes me think of those hapless relationships earlier in my life that flourished and then floundered, blossomed then withered. Life could have been quite different, if only choosing the right man had been a little easier.

Fortunately, choosing accounting software is much easier than choosing husbands. You can reduce your decision down to a series of logical questions, a simple list of features, and an analysis of the pros and cons. Oh yes, and don't worry if a product offers extra features that you don't absolutely need (after all, a man that's happy to shop as well as cook suits me just fine).

Playing with that test bunny

Looking for accounting software? Here's how to find the perfect partner for life:

- **Ask your nearest and dearest for their opinions:** Just as most mothers don't hesitate to provide incisive commentary as regards your future partner, many accountants get pretty vocal about what's best in terms of software. So, if you're tossing up between a couple of products and your accountant much prefers working with one of these in particular, you're likely to minimise accounting fees by following that recommendation.

- **Be clear about your preferences:** If Apple Macs are your thing, you're going to be unhappy crossing over to PCs. So look for accounting software willing to play on your Macintosh. (In Australia, MYOB and Xero are probably your only choices.)

- **Calculate the long-term costs:** Software companies aren't shy about their annual upgrade and/or licence fees, which often clock in at about 70 per cent of the original purchase price, payable year after year after year.

- **Find out about support:** Can you get local support and training? How many consultants nationwide support this product? If you live in the bush, find out what the local support consists of, and which product is supported best in your particular locality.

✔ **Look for a good communicator:** Nobody wants to be in a relationship with someone who only speaks in a series of grunts, so make sure your accounting software is a good communicator. Can you email invoices directly to Microsoft Outlook? Export data into other programs? Or hook up custom applications so that everyone talks to each other?

✔ **Look them up and down from head to toe:** Download product demos and put the program through its paces. (If a product doesn't offer a trial demo, give it a miss. A blind date is one thing, but life-long commitment without so much as a one-hour conversation is asking a bit much.) Focus on anything in your business that's unusual or requires special reports.

✔ **Stick to familiar ground:** If you're already accustomed to working with Quicken (a popular personal finance product), then QuickBooks makes for an easy transition. On the other hand, if you've worked in the past as a bookkeeper or accounts assistant, you're going to feel very comfortable with the more structured layout of MYOB.

✔ **Think to the future:** No, I'm not talking about the possible physical appearance of your partner in 20 years' time. I'm talking about the option to buy something relatively easy and inexpensive when you're first getting started and then upgrade to the next product in the range as your business grows.

Focusing on the pain points

When you're putting accounting software through its paces, don't focus too much on all the standard stuff such as entering transactions, reconciling bank statements or generating a Profit & Loss report. Instead, fix your beady eye on all the flash points most likely to give you (or the business that you're working for) grief:

✔ **Complex inventory:** If you're a manufacturer, wholesaler or retailer, then concentrate on the trickiest aspects of managing inventory in your business. Focus on backorder management, bills of material management, matrix pricing features, multiple warehouses, negative stock features and re-order reports.

✔ **Customer relationships:** Do you want to track prospects and customer activity and automate communications based on customer buying patterns? Then look for customer relationship management (CRM) features. Focus on ability to connect with other software applications, management reporting, remote access for salespeople in the field and email-based marketing.

✔ **Foreign costing:** Do you import or export in foreign currency? Foreign currency features in off-the-shelf accounting software products are notoriously dodgy, so test and try before you buy. Look for the ability to calculate gain or loss on foreign exchange transactions, reporting features and the ability to manage multiple currencies.

✔ **Job costing:** If a business does many jobs, and each one is unique, then sophisticated job costing features are probably the name of the game. But beware: Job costing is a real weakness with most off-the-shelf accounting products. Beware of software that doesn't let you cost labour into product manufacture, that doesn't provide salesperson reports or that can't report on jobs or projects that span financial years.

✔ **Payroll:** Three employees or more? Then you need payroll features. Ideally, look for payroll features that come as part and parcel of the accounting software, or look for payroll software that integrates easily with your accounting software. If you have many employees, look for software that caters for multiple super funds, payroll tax and multiple industrial awards.

✔ **Remote access:** Do you (or anybody else in the business for that matter) prefer to work from home, dressed in fluffy slippers and teddy-bear pyjamas? Then look for software that either operates 'in the clouds' (meaning you do your accounts online via a web browser), or that allows some other method of remote access. This way you can do the books from an office in Perth, at the same time as another employee logs in and works on reports while on a trip to New York.

✔ **Time billing:** If a business bills for time in small segments — maybe a solicitor charging by the millisecond, or an engineer accounting for time out in the field — then time billing features come in pretty handy.

Getting Down to Specifics

In Australia, the two main players are MYOB and QuickBooks, sharing up to 95 per cent of the desktop small biz accounting software market. Both products are excellent, respected worldwide and offer good local support. The upstart online product Xero is also gaining market share, and is part of a general trend towards *SaaS* — Software as a Service — products. (I readily own up to having a vested interest in both MYOB and QuickBooks. A true glutton for punishment, I'm the author of both *MYOB Software For Dummies* and *QuickBooks QBⁱ For Dummies*, Wiley Publishing Australia Pty Ltd.)

Are your eyes bigger than your stomach?

When choosing software, don't have eyes bigger than your stomach. Rather, stick to whatever level of software you need, and no more. For example, the retail price of accounting software with payroll features may not be much more than the same accounting software without payroll features. Don't think, 'Well, I may have employees someday, and the price isn't much different'. Rather, get what's needed right now, because the annual support and upgrade fees for the cheaper product are much less.

In the future, if you (or the business you work for) arrive at the point where these extra features are needed, you can simply pay a family upgrade fee.

The big questions to ask yourself when selecting accounting software are

- Do you need to manage stock levels and keep track of inventory?

- Do you need payroll? (You can get away without payroll features if you only have one or two employees, but any more employees than that, and payroll becomes essential.)

- Do you need multi-user capability, so that more than one person can use MYOB at a time?

- Do you need foreign currency features?

With your answers to these questions in mind, you're ready to assess which version is right for you.

The market gets much more fragmented for accounting software catering to medium-sized or larger businesses, and includes products such as ABM, Accomplish, Accredo, Attaché, Avanti, Microsoft Dynamics GP, Jiwa, Sage, SAP and Sybiz. I don't spend time describing these products in this chapter, because I reckon that if the job of choosing accounting software is falling on your shoulders as a bookkeeper, then you're probably working for a smaller-sized business. That's why I focus on MYOB, QuickBooks and Xero in the next few pages.

Information about accounting software dates almost as fast as my Facebook entries. So for the latest goss, make your way to the Choosing Accounting Software page of my website at www.veechicurtis.com.au.

Checking out the MYOB family

MYOB holds the lion's share of the accounting software market in both Australia and New Zealand. Its products are solid, user-friendly and offer excellent support.

The MYOB product range includes half a dozen small business products, each with a different feature set. At the entry level, you get MYOB BusinessBasics (for Windows) and FirstEdge (for Macintosh), which let you record income and expenses, and print Activity Statements. At the top level, you get the all-singing all-dancing MYOB AccountRight Enterprise, which offers accounting across multiple locations, foreign currency, complex inventory management, payroll and much more.

Personal finance software

When you set off to buy accounting software, don't get confused by the difference between small business accounting software and personal finance software.

Personal finance software is designed to help you manage household finances, home budgets and share portfolios. In contrast, small business accounting software is designed to help you bill customers, track income and expenses, manage inventory and employees, and produce essential GST reports.

The main personal finance software in Australia is Quicken Personal, which is part of the Quicken/QuickBooks range, and Stockmarket Plus, which is part of the MAUS software range.

The price ranges from about $169 for BusinessBasics to around $4,000 for AccountRight Enterprise, with nearly every price point in between. For more information, go to the Products page, and then the Accounting and Finance page, at www.myob.com.

Zooming in on QuickBooks

Although QuickBooks plays second fiddle to MYOB in Australia, QuickBooks is actually the most popular accounting software in the world, with more than 4.4 million users. This huge user base enables lots of dollars to be invested in development, resulting in a slick, user-friendly, well-designed product.

Again, I can't give you a definitive explanation of which version is best, because the decision varies according to the size and nature of your business. The QuickBooks product range includes four different small business products. QuickBooks EasyStart is the entry level product, which retails for $149 and helps manage customers, sales and expenses. At the top of the ladder is QuickBooks Enterprise, which offers everything from complex inventory to multi-currency, and retails for $2,600 (up to five users).

For more information, go to www.quicken.com.au and navigate to the Small Business page.

Going online with Xero

Xero is a relative upstart in the accounting software market, but is attracting a lot of attention and experiencing very rapid growth. Like its competitors, Xero is a complete double-entry accounting software application; unlike its competitors, Xero is one of the first companies in Australia and New Zealand to enter the market with an accounting application that is entirely online.

The look and feel of Xero is super-smart and super-cool (see Figure 4-1). All your data is online, meaning that you, the business owner or the accountant, can access info wherever you are using a Mac, a PC, an iPhone, a BlackBerry or any Windows Mobile device.

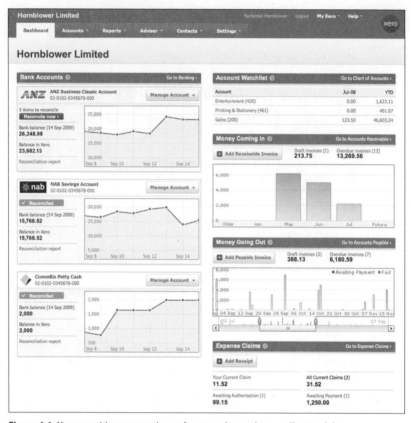

Figure 4-1: Xero provides accounting software using a clever online model.

Xero works on a subscription basis, offering three price levels, each with different features, but all including product upgrades and full technical support.

At first, the monthly subscription fees to Xero may seem a bit pricey. However, when you're weighing up costs remember that traditional off-the-shelf products not only involve a one-off purchase fee, but annual upgrade and support fees also. With some products, the annual upgrade and support fees exceed the original purchase price of the product.

For more info about Xero, visit www.xero.com.

Multi-tasking gone mad

When you start looking into acc-ounting software, you soon encounter the rather ugly term *multi-user*. This bit of computer jargon refers to the capacity of the software to let several people on a computer network work on one file at the same time. For example, if your accounting software is multi-user, one person can raise invoices, another person can record purchases and you can browse through financial reports, all at the same time.

If you think you need multi-user software, spend some time investi-gating the whole speed and networks issue. For example, although some accounting software products may say that they're multi-user, they can be slow as a wet week if you have any more than a couple of users.

Also, when comparing prices, be clear regarding the difference between a *concurrent licence* and a *unique licence*. For example, if you purchase a concurrent licence for five users, then you can load the software on as many machines as you like, but only five users can use the software at one time. If you purchase a unique licence for five users, you can only load the software on five different machines. Obviously, a concurrent licence agreement is usually more flexible and cost-effective.

Setting Up Accounting Software

The process of getting accounting software up and running can be pretty daunting. So it pays to have a plan of action and get organised.

In the next couple of pages I outline a step-by-step strategy for transforming your accounting software into a dream partner that does what it's told, is reliable and punctual, and never snores at night.

Preparing for battle

I've done literally hundreds of accounting software setups over the years, taking anything from 30 minutes for a simple service business to several days for a complex manufacturing business with 25 employees.

If you're implementing accounting software into a simple service business, preparing to go live isn't a big deal. You can simply install software at any time, pick a start date (which can be either a date that's past or a date that's some weeks ahead), and get going.

If you're implementing accounting software into a more complex business, with customer accounts, inventory or payroll, then the planning process becomes more important. I like to set a date that's some distance in the future and plan towards that, doing things like organising customer and supplier lists and the chart of accounts well in advance. Here's a step-by-step guide to help you prepare in advance.

1. **Decide on a start date.**

   Here's something I learned the hard way: The very best time of year to start off with accounting software is the beginning of the financial year (1 July for most Aussie businesses). Even if you're a few months after this date by the time you're reading this book, you're probably still best to buy accounting software now, and to go back and enter your accounts from the first day of your financial year onwards.

   Why? If you start on the first day of a new financial year, the transition from your old accounting system to your new one is a cinch, because your accountant always finalises your tax at the end of each year. You also avoid the situation where you have one set of books for part of the year and another set of books for the rest of the year, making it hard for you or your accountant to piece the whole story together.

2. **Install your accounting software.**

   Over to you. This nerdy stuff varies depending on what software you use.

3. **Work your way through the start-up interview.**

   Most accounting software offers some kind of start-up interview, with pretty simple questions such as the business name, phone numbers, legal structure and so on. Follow your nose and do your best.

   Take special care to enter the correct start date and year-end date when going through the interview. For some accounting software, this information can't be changed once set.

4. Customise your chart of accounts.

I always recommend tweaking the chart of accounts, adding accounts, changing account names or deleting accounts that you don't need. I explain all about this process in Chapter 2.

5. Create listings for customers, suppliers and items.

If you already have lists sitting elsewhere on your computer (for example, maybe you have a detailed customer listing sitting in Excel), I suggest you try to import this information rather than type it all again from scratch.

6. Customise templates for invoices, customer statements and purchase orders.

Most accounting software allows you to customise your business forms to generate personalised invoices, customer statements and so on. You may also need to customise pay advices, remittance advices and receipts.

7. As the start date approaches, make sure your paperwork is as up to date as possible.

In particular, make sure that customer accounts (recording invoices and customer payments) are up to date and the bank account is reconciled.

8. Think about how you intend to record everyday transactions, such as payments, deposits, sales and payments.

Unless you're already experienced with accounting software, make life easier for yourself by hiring a consultant to help get you started. Although training fees can be expensive, your money will be well spent.

Firing live on D-Day

Okay, so I'm assuming that you've already installed your accounting software and set up things like customer lists, accounts lists and templates (if not, refer to 'Preparing for battle' earlier in this chapter). You've arrived at 'D-Day': The date when the new accounting system is due to go live.

What happens next?

1. **Enter opening balances for customers and suppliers.**

   If you plan to use your accounting software for invoicing and you have customers that owed money as of your start date, then you need to set up opening balances for each one. The same deal applies if you want your accounting software to keep track of supplier bills — specify how much was owed to each supplier at your start date.

2. **If you have employees, set up payroll.**

   If you're going to use payroll, you're best to do so from July, as this is the beginning of the payroll year. Setting up payroll can be hideously technical and time consuming, so if you're running short of time, get some help from a consultant.

3. **If you have inventory, set up stock on hand.**

   If you want the accounting software to keep tabs on stock levels, you need to enter opening counts and cost prices for each stock item.

4. **Decide on a backup system and set it in place.**

   Backing up is important, so be sure to establish a backup system.

5. **Start entering transactions!**

   Every business is different, but I tend to start with customer invoicing (if there's no sales, there's no dosh) and customer payments, and then I move on to payroll transactions. After that, I teach bookkeepers how to record purchases and supplier payments.

When you're getting started with accounting software, don't feel you have to get everything up and running at once. Depending on the business, sometimes doing things incrementally makes sense. For example, I may start by setting up sales and inventory. Later I implement payroll, and later still, I train my clients in electronic payments and automatic remittances. I can't give a hard-and-fast rule as to what to do first, but do be careful not to bite off more than you can chew, especially if you haven't used accounting software before.

Mopping up when the dust has settled

So, you've installed the accounting software, set up lists for customers and suppliers, and started entering transactions. What comes next?

1. **Reconcile your bank account.**

   As soon as you have a month's worth of transactions, figure out how to reconcile the business bank account (and credit card accounts also, if relevant). Not sure how? Then mosey on over to Chapter 8.

2. **Put formal end-of-month or end-of-quarter procedures into place.**

   All this effort isn't worth a brass razoo unless you put procedures in place that help you double-check your work.

3. **Enter opening balances for all asset, liability and equity accounts.**

   You can't enter opening balances until the accountant has finished last year's accounts (it can take up to nine months to give birth to tax accounts), so you may be waiting several weeks, if not months, before this info is available. In the meantime, enter the balances that you know are correct, such as your bank balance, debtors, creditors and GST. The other balances can be added later.

4. **Review the state of play.**

   After a few months have passed, spend a few hours reviewing the state of play. Is the accounting system working as well as it could? Do you get all the reports you need? If not, go back to the consultant who helped you install the software, or contact the support line for the accounting software, and ask for help to ensure the system is as good as it possibly can be.

Protecting Your Accounting Data

When you record financial transactions using accounting software, the backups of the accounting software company file effectively take the place of traditional handwritten ledger books. To forget to back up is like leaving all your precious ledger books sitting out in the rain.

The accounting data backup is probably the single most important backup in any business because *all* the financial information ends up sitting in one single file, building up and up throughout the financial year until it contains a massive amount of information.

If you want to do your job well as a bookkeeper, you must aim to

✔ Back up your accounting data every time you work.

✔ Get in the habit of taking backups off-site, away from the office, so that if the office burns down or the computers are stolen, you still have your accounting data.

Although you, in your role as a bookkeeper, are probably most focused on backing up accounting data, remember that a business needs to have a backup solution for all data, including documents, emails, graphic files and so on. When deciding how to back up your accounting data, consider what other backup systems are already in place — or need to be put into place — for other business data.

Chapter 5

Understanding GST

· ·

· ·

*H*oley moley. As part of researching this chapter, I decided to download 'The Simple Guide to GST' from the Australian Taxation Office website. Many hours and 168 pages later, I was left with a strange sensation that I couldn't quite put into words.

Then in the night it came to me. *Obfuscation* was the word I was looking for. According to Wikipedia wisdom, obfuscation is the 'concealment of intended meaning in communication, making communication confusing, intentionally ambiguous and more difficult to interpret'. A more succinct definition of government-generated documents I could not imagine.

Never mind. Hopefully, the price of my suffering can be an exchange for your peace of mind. In this chapter, I take a stab at distilling how GST works, some of the do's and don'ts of accounting for GST, what mistakes to watch out for, and how to peel a grape with your tongue — no fingers or teeth allowed. (Ah, the useful skills one learns late at night in Sydney's bars.)

Coughing Up the Difference

As you probably already know, *GST* stands for *Goods and Services Tax* and is a tax that applies to most goods and services in Australia. Every time you buy a glass of wine or a new item of furniture, or you get your lawn mowed, you pay GST of 10 per cent.

As a business that's registered for GST, you pay GST on your supplies and collect GST on your sales. You have to keep a set of books that tracks how much GST you pay and how much GST you collect. If GST collected is more than GST paid, you pay this difference to the government. If GST collected is less than GST paid, you claim a refund.

For example, imagine a bookkeeper who charges a client $990 for a week's work. In that same week, the bookkeeper pays an insurance premium of $198, as well as $99 for a new laser cartridge. Figure 5-1 shows how the sums work. This bookkeeper is left with $693 in the hand after a week's work; however, the bookkeeper is now in debt to the government (aren't we all) for the difference between GST collected and GST paid. This GST equals $90 less $27, making a difference of $63 due to the government.

	Net	GST	Total
Income	900.00	90.00	990.00
Less expenses:			
Insurance	180.00	18.00	198.00
Laser cartridge for printer	90.00	9.00	99.00
	270.00	27.00	297.00
Ending Cash Balance			693.00
GST Due to Government		63.00	
Net Profit	630.00		

Figure 5-1: Calculate the difference between GST collected on sales and GST paid on purchases.

Picking a reporting method to suit

When a business registers for GST, it has to choose whether to account for GST on a cash or accrual basis.

✓ **Cash basis:** *Cash-basis* reporting means you only pay GST when you receive payments from customers and you only claim back GST when you make payments to suppliers. Note that a business can only report for GST on a cash basis if it has a turnover of less than $2 million per year.

If a business tends to owe *less* to suppliers than what customers owe to it, cash-basis reporting works best. This is the most popular method for Australian small businesses.

✓ **Accrual basis:** *Accrual-basis* reporting means you pay GST in the period that you bill the customer or receive a bill from the supplier, regardless of whether any money has exchanged hands. This approach means that if you bill a customer in March and they don't pay until July, you have to pay the GST in April regardless. Similarly, if you receive a bill from a supplier in March and you don't pay them until much later, you still claim back the GST in April.

If a business tends to owe *more* to suppliers than what customers owe to it, accrual-basis reporting works best.

You can choose to report for GST on a different basis to income tax. For example, you can choose to report for GST on a cash basis and report for tax on an accrual basis, or vice versa. Most small businesses opt to report on a cash basis for both GST and income tax purposes.

You may be feeling bamboozled by all this tax chat. No sweat — the important thing for you to realise is that any selection you make (as a business owner) or your client makes (if you're a bookkeeper) regarding the GST reporting basis or accounting basis, may have a big impact on business cashflow. If in doubt, speak to an accountant first.

Reporting for duty

If a business turns over $20 million per year or less, it can choose to report for GST on a monthly, quarterly or annual basis.

Most businesses choose to report every three months, striking a happy balance between the hassle of monthly reporting, and the psychological hurdle of only doing books once a year. The only instance that monthly reporting makes sense is for businesses that regularly receive GST refunds, such as exporters.

Calculating GST

I hope you realise that the introduction of GST heralded a major shift in the education system. Forget multiplying by two, dividing by five or understanding fractions. Cast algebra to the wind, and speak not of spelling or grammar. To get by in the world of GST, Aussie children need to be wizards at multiplying by ten and dividing by eleven. Stay cool. In the next couple of pages, I walk you through a few worked examples of how to add GST, then take it off again.

So, to calculate how much GST to add to something, simply multiply the figure by 10 per cent or 0.1. For example, if an item costs $10 and you want to find out how much GST to add, you do the following:

$$\$10 \times 0.1 = \$1$$

To add GST onto something you either add 10 per cent (using the per cent button on your calculator) or you multiply the amount by 1.1. For example, if something is $10 and you want to add 10 per cent, you do the following:

$$\$10 \times 1.1 = \$11$$

If an amount already includes GST, and you want to calculate the GST component, you simply divide the amount by 11. For example, if you buy something for $110 and you want to figure how much GST is in the total, you do the following:

$$\$110 \div 11 = \$10$$

To figure out what the cost of this item was before GST was added, you divide the total cost by 1.1. For example, if you buy something for $110 and you want to figure out how much this item cost before GST, you do the following:

$$\$110 \div 1.1 = \$100$$

Fortunately, most accounting software calculates GST automatically. With both MYOB and QuickBooks you can choose to enter prices either excluding or including tax (for example, in MYOB, you make this selection by toggling the Tax Inclusive button; in QuickBooks, you toggle the Amounts Include Tax button). Then, as soon you enter a tax code, the software automatically calculates the tax. Sweet as a nut.

Figuring What's Taxed and What's Not

When you talk about whether GST applies to stuff, or not, you get four different scenarios.

- ✔ **Scenario number one:** Regular GST, which you either pay or you get charged, and which you report on your Business Activity Statement (BAS). Most transactions fall into this category. For more details, skip ahead to 'Move it, groove it, tax it'.

- ✔ **Scenario number two:** GST isn't charged or claimed but you have to report it on your BAS. For example, you don't charge GST on exports, but you do have to report all export income. For more details, skip ahead to 'Transactions with no GST'.

- ✔ **Scenario number three:** In this scenario, you don't charge GST or pay GST and you don't report it either. For more details, skip ahead to 'Transactions with no GST'.

- ✔ **Scenario number four:** In this scenario, the supplier charges GST but you can't claim it. This applies if you aren't registered for GST, but the supplier is, or if you're a landlord of residential real estate and you can't claim back the GST on related purchases. For more details, skip ahead to 'Transactions with no GST'.

Bank charges and interest

Bank charges and interest expense are GST-free, which means you don't claim GST on either expense, but you report these transactions on your Business Activity Statement.

Move it, groove it, tax it

Almost as certain as death and as painful as unrequited love, most things get taxed. In Australia, where the love of inefficient bureaucracy and red tape betrays a colonial legacy, a flat GST of 10 per cent applies to most goods and services, but with a long list of exceptions. You know, a bottle of orange juice from a supermarket doesn't have GST, but a bottle of orange juice from a takeaway café does; bandages and band-aids don't have GST, but tampons most certainly do (at this point, does one detect patriarchal as well as colonial influences at work?).

I'll cut to the chase. As a bookkeeper, if you're doing the books for a business that's registered for GST, then you need to keep track of two things: How much GST you collect on sales, and how much GST you pay out on purchases. If you do handwritten books or use a spreadsheet, you track GST by creating a separate column for tax. If you use accounting software, you have a special code for each transaction that indicates the tax status.

But there's an added complication (of course!). If a business buys capital items over $100 (or $1,000 if a business is eligible for small business entity tax concessions), you have to report these purchases separately on your BAS.

Transactions with no GST

Transactions that don't attract GST fall into three categories:

 ✔ Transactions that are GST-free that you report on your BAS

✔ Transactions that are input-taxed that you report on your BAS

✔ Transactions that don't attract GST and that you don't report on your BAS

I expand a little on each of these categories in the headings below.

Transactions that are GST-free that you report on your BAS

GST-free transactions are transactions where you don't charge for GST on sales or pay GST on purchases, but you report separately for these sales or purchases in your BAS.

GST-free transactions include childcare, educational courses, essential non-processed foods, export sales and medical supplies.

Transactions that are input-taxed that you report on your BAS

Another type of income and expense that has no GST, but you still need to report, is income and expenses relating to residential properties. As a landlord, you can't charge GST on rent, nor can you claim GST on rent-related expenses. This kind of income is called *input-taxed income*, and the related expenses are called *input-taxed purchases*.

Income from interest and dividends is also input taxed.

Transactions that don't attract GST and that you don't report on your BAS

This third category covers all transactions that don't attract GST, but that you also don't report on your BAS. These transactions include

✔ Internal transactions within a business, such as cash transfers, depreciation, transfers between accounts, movements in stock and loan repayments

✔ Payments of tax itself (there is no GST on GST ... yet!)

✔ Personal spending or drawings or owner's contributions

✔ Wages and superannuation

Trading with non-registered suppliers

If you're registered for GST but a business that you purchase supplies from isn't, you treat the goods or services that you buy from this supplier as being GST-free. You include these transactions on your BAS worksheet, in box G14.

Setting Up Tax Codes in Accounting Software

Earlier in this chapter, I explain that you get four scenarios with GST: Sales or purchases *with* GST that you report on your BAS; sales or purchases *without* GST that you also report on your BAS; sales or purchases *without* GST that you *don't* report on your BAS and last, sales and purchases where you get charged GST but can't claim it. When you work with accounting software, you need a tax code for each of these scenarios, plus a couple more besides.

In the next few pages, I explain how to set up tax codes, and then how to link the accounts in your chart of accounts to these tax codes. (Refer to Chapter 2 for more on the chart of accounts.)

Creating a list of tax codes

Here's a quick-and-dirty summary of how to set up tax codes for both MYOB and QuickBooks. Other accounting software may have slightly different approaches, but the principles are the same regardless of what software you use.

1. **Make sure you have a tax code for GST sales and purchases.**

   In MYOB, this code is simply GST. In QuickBooks, this code is GST; or alternatively, NCG (for GST on Purchases) and GST (for GST on Sales). By the way, in QuickBooks, you also need to customise a tax items list so that QuickBooks knows how to report tax codes on your BAS. For more details, refer to my tome *QuickBooks QB[i] For Dummies* or refer to QuickBooks help.

2. **Create a code for GST purchases that are also capital acquisitions.**

   I talk more about capital acquisitions earlier in this chapter in the section 'Move it, groove it, tax it'. In MYOB, this code is usually either CAP or GCA. In QuickBooks, this code can be either CAP or CAG.

3. **Create another code for items that are GST-free.**

   In MYOB, this code is simply FRE. In QuickBooks, this code can be either FRE, or NCF (for GST-free purchases) and FRE (for GST-free sales).

4. **Now create a tax code for input-taxed sales and, if necessary, another for input-taxed purchases.**

   Input-taxed sales is a fancy name for interest income, dividend income or residential income. In both MYOB and QuickBooks, I use the code ITS for input-taxed sales. For expenses that relate directly to input-taxed sales (property expenses, for example), I use a code called INP.

5. **Last, create a code for non-reportable transactions.**

   In MYOB, the N-T code is the one to use for non-reportable transactions. Because MYOB uses N-T as the default, this tax code automatically comes up on transactions unless you select something else.

   In QuickBooks, I suggest you create a new tax code called NR for non-reportable transactions. Some people don't bother using any code for non-reportable transactions in QuickBooks, but I don't recommend this method. Unless you enter a tax code for every transaction, it gets tricky to distinguish between transactions where you have forgotten to enter a tax code and transactions that you know are non-reportable or exempt.

6. **Do a pirouette or two, then see if your list of tax codes looks anything like Figure 5-2.**

   I show the QuickBooks tax code list in Figure 5-2, but the tax code list in MYOB looks much the same.

Code	Description	Taxable
CAG	Cap. Acq. - Inc GST	✓
FRE	GST Free Supplies	✓
GST	10% GST	✓
INP	Input Taxed Sales	✓
NR	Not Reportable	

Tax Code ▼   Activities ▼   Reports ▼   ☐ Include inactive

Figure 5-2: Setting up tax codes.

The list I show in Figure 5-2 is perfect for 99 per cent of businesses. However, some businesses may need additional tax codes, specifically if you (or the business you're working for) are required to report for ABN withholding tax, export sales, luxury car tax, voluntary wine equalisation tax or withholding tax. If any of these taxes apply, get advice from your accountant.

Linking accounts to tax codes

The secret to producing an accurate BAS is to get the tax code right on every transaction. In both MYOB and QuickBooks, you can make this process pretty easy by linking each account in your chart of accounts with a specific tax code. (For more about building your chart of accounts, refer to Chapter 2.)

You can see how this works in Figure 5-3, where I show a typical chart of accounts from MYOB. Obviously, the format of this chart varies depending on whether you use MYOB or QuickBooks but the concept is the same: Because each account is linked to a specific tax code, the correct code comes up every time you select an account. For example, if the tax code for Advertising Expense is GST, then every time you allocate a payment transaction to Advertising Expense, GST pops up automatically as the tax code. (In MYOB, you can link tax codes to every account; in QuickBooks, you can link tax codes to income, cost of sales and expense accounts only.)

All Accounts	Asset	Liability	Equity	Income	Cost of Sales	Expense	Other Income	Other Expense

Account Name			Type	Tax	Linked	Balance
⇨ 6-0000	**Expenses**		Expense			$132,323.73 ▲
⇨ 6-1000	**General & Admin Expenses**		Expense			$15,397.46
⇨	6-1100	Accounting Fees	Expense	GST		$2,949.91
⇨	6-1110	Advertising	Expense	GST		$9,899.36
⇨	6-1120	Bad Debts	Expense	GST		$0.00
⇨	6-1130	Bank Charges	Expense	FRE		$132.76
⇨	6-1140	Depreciation	Expense	N-T		$100.00
⇨	6-1150	Discounts Taken	Expense	GST	✓	$0.00
⇨	6-1155	Donations	Expense	FRE		$0.00
⇨	6-1160	Freight Paid	Expense	GST	✓	$0.00
⇨	6-1180	Office Supplies	Expense	GST		$1,568.91
⇨	6-1190	Other General Expenses	Expense	QUE		$0.00
⇨	6-1200	Subscriptions	Expense	GST		$364.52
⇨	6-1210	Repairs & Maintenance	Expense	GST		$31.82
⇨	6-1217	Motor Vehicle Repairs & Maint	Expense	GST		$350.18
⇨	6-1218	Motor Vehicle Registration	Expense	FRE		$0.00
⇨ 6-2000	**Operating Expenses**		Expense			$19,530.56
⇨	6-2110	Cleaning	Expense	GST		$135.01
⇨	6-2120	Electricity	Expense	GST		$2,393.07
⇨	6-2125	Gas	Expense	GST		$2,827.74
⇨	6-2130	Insurance	Expense	GST		$1,561.35 ▼

↑ Up   ↓ Down   Combine Accounts

Help F1   Print   New   Budgets   Edit   Close

Figure 5-3: Configure your chart of accounts so that each account corresponds to the correct tax code.

The implications are huge: If you set up the correct tax code for every account in your chart of accounts correctly, right from the start, you're almost guaranteed of coding all your transactions right, every time. Perfection and nirvana are but moments away.

Staying Out of Trouble

I have a sister who is a tax auditor specialising in big-time customs fraud. She's relatively high up these days, and she spends most of her time interviewing the underworld individuals who make the baddies in a James Bond movie look like kittens. 'Interrogations', she likes to call these interviews, with a steely glint in her eye and a tightening of the upper lip.

I imagine that 99.99 per cent of the bookkeepers reading this book have nothing to fear from a fraud investigation, even if conducted by my fearsome sister. However, the dread of a tax audit looms high for even the most conscientious of bookkeepers. Usually, the fear isn't so much that an auditor finds that you've consciously covered up income or over-claimed something like GST refunds, rather the fear is that you've made a mistake by accident and now you'll get into trouble.

So in the interests of making sure you get a good night's sleep, year in year out, I provide a few handy hints for getting everything just right.

Avoiding traps for the unwary

So you know the theory, and now you're responsible for deciphering the tax status of hundreds of transactions. What are the most common mistakes to look out for?

- ✓ **Bank fees and merchant fees:** Bank fees are GST-free, but merchant fees and the hire of EFTPOS machines attracts GST.

- ✓ **Government charges:** Council rates, filing fees, land tax, licence renewals, motor vehicle rego and stamp duty are all GST-free.

- ✓ **Insurance:** Almost every insurance policy is a mixture of being taxable and GST-free (stamp duty doesn't have GST on it). Don't get caught out. Instead, double-check the exact amount of GST on every single insurance payment.

- ✓ **Loan payments and hire purchase:** You can't claim GST on loan payments, nor can you claim GST on the total amount of hire purchase payments. With hire purchase, the correct treatment is either to claim the whole amount of GST when you originally purchase the asset, or to claim the GST progressively on each payment, splitting up the interest and the principal. (Clear as mud? Ask your accountant for advice.)

- ✓ **Overseas travel:** Overseas travel is GST-free, meaning that you must report the expense, but no GST applies.

✔ **Personal stuff:** You can't claim the full amount of GST on expenses that are partly personal — motor vehicle and home office expenses are the obvious culprits. (See the later section 'Keeping personal matters separate' for more details.)

✔ **Petty cash:** Petty cash is usually a mixed bag. Coffee and tea are GST-free, biscuits and sticky-tape aren't.

✔ **Small suppliers:** Watch out for small suppliers who have an ABN but aren't registered for GST. Record these purchases as GST-free.

✔ **Tax Invoices:** You can't claim GST on any amount over $82.50 (GST-inclusive) unless you have a Tax Invoice. (But remember that in any case, you need a copy of every single receipt and invoice for income tax purposes.)

Keeping personal matters separate

If a business owner purchases goods or services that they use partly for private purposes, then be careful not to claim the GST on the private component.

For example, if you (or the business owner) claim your motor vehicle as a business expense, but your logbook shows that 20 per cent of use is actually personal, then you can only claim 80 per cent of the GST when you record the transaction. For example, Figure 5-4 shows how Maryanne pays for motor vehicle repairs on her Mercedes sports car. The total bill is for $1,000 but when she records the payment, she only allocates $800 to Motor Vehicle Repairs, allocating the remaining $200 to Personal Drawings.

The other approach is to claim the whole amount of GST with every transaction and request the accountant make an adjustment at the end of the financial year. This method works okay, but isn't quite as accurate as recording transactions correctly throughout the year, and may of course cost the business a tad extra in accounting fees.

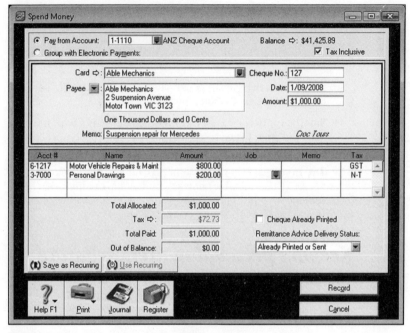

Figure 5-4: Apportioning personal expenses.

Dancing the Paperwork Polka

As soon as you register for GST, you need to make sure that every invoice you supply to customers includes certain key information, such as your business name, your ABN, the date and so on. In turn, you need to keep a beady eye on your suppliers' bills so that they do the same, providing you with all the info you need in order to be able to claim GST back from your payments to them.

Riveting stuff? I'm on the edge of my seat as well. Read on for a detailed checklist of what's required.

Brewing Up a Tax Invoice

If you're registered for GST and you send a client an invoice that's for more than $75 before GST, then you must issue a Tax Invoice. The invoice needs to include the following:

- ✔ Your Australian Business Number (ABN) and your business or trading name. Because an invoice is essentially a contract, the legal beagles recommend you stick this info at the very top of each invoice, above the details of what it is that you're selling.

- ✔ The words 'Tax Invoice' written clearly in nice big letters on the first page of the invoice.

- ✔ The date.

- ✔ A brief description of whatever it is that you're supplying.

- ✔ If the invoice is for taxable goods or services only, you need to either show the total amount of GST payable or add a comment saying that the total price includes GST.

- ✔ If the invoice is for a mix of taxable and non-taxable goods, clearly identify each item that's taxable and show exactly how much GST is payable.

If an invoice comes to more than $1,000 (including GST), you need to include some additional info:

- ✔ You also need to include either your customer's name and address or your customer's name and ABN.

- ✔ Invoices over $1,000 must include the quantity or volume of whatever it is that you're supplying. For example, the number of hours charged, or the number of units supplied.

Generating invoices for your customers

Sometimes it's more convenient for the business receiving goods or services to calculate how much something is worth and generate an invoice. For example, my publisher pays me royalties based on book sales. I don't send my publisher an invoice, but instead, my publisher generates an invoice on my behalf. This invoice is just the same as a Tax Invoice except that it has the words 'Recipient Created Tax Invoice' (now there's a sexy bit of jargon), printed at the top.

You can see a typical Tax Invoice in Figure 5-5.

White Water Guides

ABN 99 009 080 333

TAX INVOICE   20/08/09

Katy Lewis
2 Paradise Way
Utopia 2777

White water rafting trip, Nymph river	$200.00
Travel and refreshments	$ 30.00
SUBTOTAL	**$230.00**
Add GST @ 10 %	$ 23.00
TOTAL including GST	**$253.00**

www.whitewaterguides.net.au PO BOX 1228, Kellyville, NSW 2050, 02 4737 9999

Figure 5-5: A typical Tax Invoice.

Tax Invoices don't need to be complicated documents. So long as you include the bare legal information I outline, a Tax Invoice can be as simple as a cash register docket, a hand-written scrap of paper or a short and tender email.

Checking supplier bills

In the same way as you're responsible for making sure that you issue legit Tax Invoices to customers, you also need to make sure that your supplier bills toe the line.

Make sure that supplier bills include the supplier's ABN, an accurate description, the date and the total amount payable. If the supplier is registered for GST, the invoice should also say 'Tax Invoice' at the top, and either a statement that GST is included or a subtotal showing the amount of GST charged. Last, any invoice over $1,000 needs to show the quantity or volume of the goods or services supplied, such as litres of petrol or hours of labour.

If you operate under a company structure, make sure that whenever you (or the business owner) purchase new business equipment, the bill is made out to the company name and not to an individual name. Tax auditors are always on the lookout for 'other' bills, and bills made out to individuals aren't deductible as company expenses.

Most suppliers include these details on bills as a matter of course. However, watch out for incidental receipts, and stay tuned to the fact that the slip of paper you get when you pay for something by credit card or EFTPOS is often separate to the receipt itself. This kind of docket, which usually just shows the date and the total amount paid, isn't a legitimate receipt as far as your tax is concerned. (I guess the tax auditors are trying to cover for all those situations where someone buys $40 of petrol on their credit card and then chucks in a couple of Paddle Pops for the kids on top.)

Paying GST

Reporting for GST tends to be a tyranny of existence for most bookkeepers. Everything else can fall behind, but the date for submitting your BAS is set in stone. If you don't make the date, then before you know it, a personalised love letter arrives from the powers that be, complete with a substantial fine.

So grab your calendar and read on ...

Meeting deadlines

So how often do you have to report for GST? Depending on the size of your business and what choices you make when you register, you have to submit reports monthly, quarterly or annually (for more about this choice, head back to the 'Reporting for duty' section earlier in this chapter). Most businesses choose to report quarterly.

However, calculating your true 'deadline' can be a tricky business.

✔ If you pay monthly, your deadline is 21 days after the end of each month.

✔ If you pay quarterly, your deadline is 28 days after the end of each quarter, except for the second quarter of the year (October to December) when you get an extra four weeks.

✔ If you lodge activity statements electronically using the Tax Office portal, you automatically get a two-week extension on the due date.

✔ If you get your accountant to lodge activity statements electronically, you get a handsome four-week extension.

Even if you're strapped for cash, lodge your activity statement anyway. (The Tax Office only issues fines for lodging forms late, it doesn't issue fines for paying late. The only punishment administered is an interest charge for late payments.) For most businesses, so long as you pay within a couple of weeks of lodging the form, the Tax Office won't so much as blink an eye. If you can't pay within a couple of weeks, contact the Tax Office and request a payment extension.

Managing cashflow

Even though the fun and games of sending in activity statements occurs only every couple of months, you may prefer to put money aside on a much more regular basis. This way, you can be confident that you have enough cash by the time the deadlines strikes.

So, if you're on the hunt for a stress-free existence, follow these steps.

1. **Keep accounts up to date.**

   Dull, I know. But unless you're up to date recording sales and expenses, how else can you figure out where you stand with GST?

2. **Print a GST report at the end of each month.**

   Notice how the report in Figure 5-6 summarises both GST collected and paid? I used MYOB software to produce this report, but you can get the same information using any accounting software.

3. **Subtract the amount of GST you pay from the amount of GST you collect.**

   The difference between these two figures is the amount of GST you owe.

4. **Calculate how much tax you withheld from employee wages for the month.**

   Look up how much tax you deducted from employee wages — if any.

5. **Look up previous activity statements to see whether you're up for any additional taxes this month.**

   For example, you may have to pay PAYG instalment tax or fringe benefits tax in addition to GST and PAYG withholding tax.

6. **Total the amounts that you calculated in Steps 3–5 above.**

7. **Transfer the total amount from Step 6 into a savings account.**

8. **Sleep well ... no nasty surprises waiting around the corner.**

   With the exception of those four, big green bogeymen, of course.

GST [Summary - Accrual]

1/03/2009 To 31/03/2009

Page 1

Code	Description	Rate	Sale Value	Purchase Value	Tax Collected	Tax Paid
EXP	GST Free Exports	0.000%	$2,500.00			
FRE	GST Free	0.000%	$402.00	$1,242.00		
GST	Goods & Services Tax	10.000%	$20,425.00	$18,722.00	$1,856.82	$1,702.00
N-T	Not Reportable	0.000%		$275.00		
				Total:	$1,856.82	$1,702.00

Figure 5-6: Print reports regularly to find out how much GST you owe.

Astral travel through the portal

If you're a BAS service provider, the Tax Agent Portal is a pretty nifty way for you to communicate with the Tax Office. With the portal, you can lodge activity statements for clients, view or change previously lodged activity statements, and add or delete clients from your client directory.

When it comes time to pay, you can check out payment options, download BAS payment forms, and communicate with the Tax Office using secure portal mail. For more information, visit the Tax Agent Portal page at www.ato.gov.au.

Part III

Recording Day-to-Day Transactions

Glenn Lumsden

'Let's see, you were five minutes late,
then you worked back twenty, then
I gave you a free lunch, then you
were on the phone for two minutes ...
let's call it $50 cash.'

In this part ...

This part of the book arrives at the heart of the matter: Recording income, entering expenses, and reconciling bank accounts. These everyday transactions form the bread and butter of every bookkeeper's existence. After all, what's more important than cataloguing money in and money out, and calculating how much is left in the honey pot at the day's end?

But after you've entered all the details, then what? Time to create some financial reports. These reports enable you to answer important questions such as 'What is my net worth?' (Nothing to do with self-esteem, I can assure you.) Or 'Am I making enough money to afford a new yacht and a month in the Whitsundays?' (Please do send me an invitation if you are.)

If you're anxious about working with financial reports, don't be. I devote all of Chapter 9 to explaining how to interpret these reports and check that the figures are correct.

Chapter 6

Recording Expenses and Payments

· ·

In This Chapter

▶ Finding homes for all your bits of paper

▶ Choosing a method to set up your books

▶ Guarding that petty cash tin with fire in the belly and a glint in the eye

▶ Allocating every transaction to its correct account

▶ Getting technical with accrual accounting (purchase orders, supplier bills and more)

· ·

*I*n this chapter, I arrive at the heart of the matter, explaining how to record expenses and supplier payments. I start by exploring the innards of a simple handwritten cash journal (after all, bookkeepers have used this method for hundreds of years), but I quickly move on to demonstrate the same activities using a spreadsheet or accounting software.

A simple cash payments journal (whether handwritten or computerised) works well for many different businesses, but if you want to keep tabs on inventory or maintain a set of books that shows how much you owe to suppliers, then accrual accounting is the name of the game. I explain how this deal works towards the end of the chapter.

Keep in mind that a good bookkeeper is smart, organised and just a tad pedantic (not to mention good-looking and blindingly intelligent). A smart bookkeeper looks for ways to improve systems and make clever use of technology. An organised bookkeeper transforms a chaos of paperwork into a set of logical files where anyone can find anything. And a slightly pedantic bookkeeper takes care when allocating transactions, choosing expense accounts with precision and asking questions when in doubt.

Creating Order Out of Chaos

For every bookkeeper, the starting point for cataloguing expenses is always the *source documents* of a business. When accountants talk about source documents, they mean bank statements, chequebooks, credit card statements, receipts and supplier bills.

Your first job is to gather all these source documents together into one place and whistle 'em into order:

- ✔ **Bank statements:** I prefer to work from printed bank statements sent to me from my bank, rather than from statements printed from my internet banking (because internet banking often prints transactions with the most recent transaction first, which I find confusing). I suggest you store bank statements in a ring binder (with a new ring binder for every financial year), with coloured dividers separating each bank account. Keep bank statements in date order, with the most recent statements on top.

- ✔ **Chequebooks:** Does anybody write cheques anymore? If your answer is yes, make sure you have the most recent chequebooks to hand, and write the start date and the bank account on the front of each one.

- ✔ **Credit card statements:** I treat credit card statements in the same way as any other bank statement, filing them in date order in the bank statement ring binder.

- ✔ **Receipts:** Separate receipts into two piles: One pile for everything that was paid for by cash, and another pile for everything that was paid by cheque, electronic transfer or credit card. The cash receipts need extra attention — see 'Nitpicking over Petty Cash' later in this chapter for more details. The other receipts simply need filing away (the best method is usually to file receipts under supplier name, sorted within each supplier in date order, with the most recent receipt on top).

- ✔ **Supplier bills:** If a supplier bill hasn't been paid yet, pop this bill into a folder marked 'Bills to be Paid'. If a bill has been paid, file it away with all your other bills in a folder with that supplier's name.

Recording Payments — Three Methods

So you have your bank statements, chequebooks, receipts and bills all close to hand. You're ready to create your first set of books.

Although the principles of bookkeeping stay constant whatever method you use, the practicalities vary depending whether you do a set of books by hand, use a spreadsheet or work with accounting software. In this chapter, I don't attempt to discuss the pros and cons of each method (that's what Chapter 4 is all about), but instead I explore all three methods, outlining a plan of attack for each one.

Writing a journal by hand

In Figure 6-1 you can see a typical handwritten *payments journal*, a set of accounts listing business outgoings. This journal takes a typical format, listing transactions in date order, showing the amount including GST in the Amount column, followed by the tax in the GST column, and the net value of the payment in the relevant expense column.

Payments Journal

Number	Date	Description	Amount	GST	Purchases	Bank Fees	Computer	Motor Vehicle	Wages	Wages Tax	Transfers
Chq 1023	2/10/2010	Supplies for resale	1,100.00	100.00	1,000.00						
Bank fee	2/10/2010	Bank fee	12.00			12.00					
eft	3/10/2010	Pam Pilot - Wages	750.00						850.00	- 100.00	
Chq 1024	4/10/2010	Supplies for resale	350.00	31.82	318.18						
eft	4/10/2010	DextraCable - New cabling	280.00	25.45			254.55				
eft	4/10/2010	Transfer to savings	1,000.00								1,000.00
Lease	5/10/2010	Westpac Vehicle Lease	660.00	60.00				600.00			
eft	6/10/2010	Able Motor Repairs	190.00	17.27				172.73			
eft	6/10/2010	Pam Pilot - Wages	750.00						850.00	- 100.00	
		Totals	5,092.00	234.55	1,318.18	12.00	254.55	772.73	1,700.00	- 200.00	1,000.00

Figure 6-1: A typical handwritten payments journal.

You can probably make a stab at doing a payments journal just by buying a ledger book from the newsagent and copying this format, but I'll chuck a few comments into the mix to help you along:

1. **Do a separate page (or set of pages) for each bank account.**

   Why? You find out later (Chapter 8 to be precise), when you use the totals from this journal to reconcile your bank account.

2. **List transactions in date order.**

   In years gone by, I used to list transactions by working from the cheque stubs in each chequebook, because this was the only way to make sure I listed transactions in date order (and indeed, for businesses that still write numerous cheques, I still prefer to work this way). Nowadays, I find it easiest to refer directly to bank statements, because most businesses tend to pay using electronic transfer rather than cheques, quickly double-checking at the end of each statement that there aren't any cheques that have been written, but that haven't cleared yet.

3. **Show GST in a separate column.**

   Note that in Figure 6-1 bank charges, wages and account transfers don't have any GST on them.

4. **Record the amount of each expense without GST included in the relevant expense column.**

   For example, the first line of Figure 6-2 shows a $110 payment for advertising. I write $110 in the Amount column, $10 in the GST column and $100 in the Adverts column. You can name these expense columns whatever you like but if you run out of room (maybe your journal book doesn't have enough columns), then create a column at the end called 'Other Expenses'. Use this column for miscellaneous expenses that don't crop up very often.

5. **Total each column.**

   At this point, handwritten books get pretty painful. Yep, you have to grab your calculator and total each column.

6. **Double-check that the totals match.**

   More fun and games. Add up the total of the GST column and all the columns to the right of that column (Adverts,

Bank Fees and so on), and write this total on the bottom line in the far-right column (in Figure 6-1, this total is $5,092). Compare this total to the total of the Amount column. The two figures should match!

What if they don't? Then pause, eat some chocolate, have a cup of tea and start again, double-checking every total. The mistake is there somewhere, just waiting for you to find.

Getting smart with a spreadsheet

When writing about using spreadsheets to do your books, I can't be that specific about what method to use. Because spreadsheets are such a do-it-yourself method, people seem to have different approaches. Some people use spreadsheets in exactly the same format as traditional handwritten books. Other nerdy folk develop all-singing, all-dancing spreadsheets that generate invoices, calculate total expenses and produce colourful Profit & Loss reports to boot (but which require a master's degree in programming).

In Figure 6-2, I show one possible format for a spreadsheet journal. You can see that this spreadsheet looks pretty similar to Figure 6-1, but with one notable exception: I include both receipts and payments on the same worksheet. The logic behind this method is that I can also include a running bank account balance, making it super easy to spot mistakes or missing entries. (You can create a running balance on a spreadsheet using formulas, whereas with handwritten books a running balance would involve too many calculations.)

Number	Date	Description	Amount In	Amount Out	GST Collected	GST Paid	Adverts	Bank Fees	Computer	Motor Vehicle	Sales with GST	Sales no GST	Bank Balance
		Opening bank balance											1,250.00
Chq 1023	2/10/2010	Gazette (advertising)		110.00		10.00	100.00						1,140.00
Inv 212	2/10/2010	Sale to T Stubbs	1,300.00		118.18						1,181.82		2,440.00
Bank fee	2/10/2010	Bank fee		12.00				12.00					2,428.00
Inv 213	3/10/2010	Sale to A Wilson	1,100.00		100.00						1,000.00		3,528.00
Chq 1024	4/10/2010	Integral Energy		350.00		31.82							3,178.00
eft	4/10/2010	DextraCable - New cabling		280.00		25.45			254.55				2,898.00
Lease	5/10/2010	Westpac Vehicle Lease		660.00		60.00				600.00			2,238.00
Interest	6/10/2010	Bank Interest	22.50									22.50	2,260.50
eft	6/10/2010	Able Motor Repairs		190.00		17.27				172.73			2,070.50
		Totals	2,422.50	1,602.00	218.18	144.55	100.00	12.00	254.55	772.73	2,181.82	22.50	

Figure 6-2: Creating a payments journal using a spreadsheet.

So you're game to have a go? Here are some tips to help you on your way:

1. **Create a new spreadsheet, name it something sensible and store it in a folder where you can find it.**

   Yeah, yeah. All obvious stuff, but you're about to invest hours and hours working with this little number, so store the spreadsheet file somewhere where you can find it, give it a sensible name and, if anybody else can access your computer, add a password to protect the file.

2. **If you need to, create a separate sheet for each bank account.**

   Can you see that there are three tabs along the bottom of Figure 6-2? One for the cheque account, one for the savings account and one for the credit card account.

3. **Set up columns similar to Figure 6-2, with separate columns for the total amount, for GST, and for each expense and income category.**

   I doubt you want to read this Dummies book with a magnifying glass, so I don't include many columns in my example. But you can create as many columns as your heart desires.

4. **Set up formulas to calculate GST.**

   This is a book about bookkeeping, not an Excel manual, so you're on your own when it comes to in-depth formulas and the like. But I'll give you a tip: The formula in the first row of my journal in my GST Paid column is $= G6/11$.

Bank charges (and other tragic facts of life)

I like to separate bank charges into two accounts, one called Bank Fees and another — if relevant — called Merchant Fees. (Your bank only charges merchant fees if you offer credit card facilities to customers.) The reason I separate transactions into two accounts is that, while regular bank fees don't attract GST, EFTPOS and merchant fees do. In addition, I create a third account called Interest Expense (interest also doesn't attract GST).

5. **Enter data, using formulas to calculate amounts after GST.**

   For example, the first transaction listed in this journal is an advertising payment for $110. The formula in the Adverts column is = **E6–G6**, which equals the figure in the Amount column less the figure in the GST Paid column.

6. **At the end of each month, insert totals at the bottom of each column.**

   My example only shows a week's worth of transactions, but in practice you usually insert totals at the end of each month. Use the Sum command to add up each column. (Not sure how? I can recommend an excellent guide called — guess what? *Excel 2010 For Dummies*, of course. Books for earlier versions of the Excel software are also available.)

7. **Enter the opening balance of your bank account, and set up a formula to calculate the running balance.**

   I love this running balance trick. I enter my opening bank balance on the first line of the cash journal, and after that, I get Excel to calculate the running balance automatically. In my spreadsheet, I use the formula = **P5+D6–E6** on the first line (opening bank balance plus money in, less money out), and then I copy that formula all the way down.

8. **Match the running balance column with your bank statement.**

   Matching this balance against your bank statement is the litmus test that you've recorded everything correctly. If it matches, you're a hero! If it doesn't, you need to find out where you've made your mistake.

9. **Back up or die.**

   Need I say more?

With this spreadsheet, because I list transactions in date order according to when they appear on the bank statement, I don't include any *unpresented cheques* (cheques which have been written but which haven't been cashed yet). From an accounting perspective, this tactic isn't strictly accurate, because a cheque counts as an expense the moment you pop the envelope in the post, rather than the moment it clears from your bank account. My workaround? Whenever I draw up a set of financial reports, or prepare final end-of-year accounts for tax purposes, I simply add any unpresented cheques to the list of transactions.

Staying sweet with accounting software

In Chapter 3, I talk about a delightful chap called Pacioli, who way back in 1494 invented this double-entry bookkeeping caper that we know and love so well. At the beginning of this chapter, I explain how to write up a payments journal by hand, using a method that hasn't changed much since Pacioli's time.

If you use accounting software to record your payments, you may be surprised to find out that Pacioli's principles are still in full swing. For example, if you look at a typical Bank Register in QuickBooks (as per Figure 6-3) you can see that the format isn't wildly different from the handwritten ledger back in Figure 6-1.

Date	Number	Payee		Payment	✓	Deposit	Balance
Ex.Rate	Type	Account	Memo				
30/09/2010		Acmer Pty Ltd				6,396.00	1,250.00
	RCPT	-split-					
02/10/2010		Terrence Stubbs				1,300.00	2,550.00
	RCPT	-split-					
02/10/2010	Fee	Westpac		12.00			2,538.00
	CHQ	Bank Service Charges	Bank fee				
02/10/2010	1023	Gazette		110.00			2,428.00
	CHQ	-split-	Advert feature for Janurary				
03/10/2010		Andy Wilson				1,100.00	3,528.00
	RCPT	-split-					
04/10/2010	eft	DextraCable		280.00			3,248.00
	CHQ	Repairs:Computer Repairs	New cabling ADSL				
04/10/2010	1024	Integral Energy		350.00			2,898.00
	CHQ	-split-	August bill				
05/10/2010	Lease	Westpac		660.00			2,238.00
	CHQ	Motor Expense	Lease Payment				
06/10/2010						22.50	2,260.50
	DEP	Interest Income	Deposit				
06/10/2010	eft	Able Motor Repairs		190.00			2,070.50
	CHQ	-split-	New starter motor				
06/10/2010	1025	Payee		Payment		Deposit	
		Account	Memo				

Ending balance 2,070.50

Figure 6-3: Entering transactions using QuickBooks.

I can't be too specific about the mechanics of creating a payments journal using accounting software, because the method varies depending what software you use. You can pick up one of the other books I've done for Wiley — *MYOB Software For Dummies* or *QuickBooks QB^i For Dummies* — if you really want to know.

Traditional bookkeeping turned on its head

Most accounting software now enables you to record supplier payments and then either use the accounting software to process these payments, or create a supplier payments file that you can then send to your internet banking software.

This approach turns traditional bookkeeping on its head. No longer do you work from source documents such as chequebooks and credit card statements, referring to these documents in order to do your books. Instead you use the accounting software itself as the tool to make the payments.

The level of sophistication in this process depends on the accounting software. The most common method of working is to record supplier payments in the software, and then create a bank file that summarises

these payments. Next, you fire up your online banking software, open up the summary payment file you just created and confirm your payment instructions. Last, you return to your accounting software to create remittance advices which you then post, email or fax to suppliers.

An alternative approach (the one favoured by MYOB software) is to roll the accounting software and internet banking into one. With this method, you record supplier payments into MYOB, then authorise the payment using MYOB's banking gateway. At the point you authorise a payment, funds transfer from your bank account to your supplier's account, and the supplier automatically receives an email or a fax notifying them of this payment.

However, for some general tips about recording payments using accounting software, read on.

1. **Enter transactions using a method that fits the way you think.**

   I'm sounding pretty vague here, I confess. But with both MYOB and QuickBooks, for example, you can choose between recording transactions straight into the Bank Register or recording transactions using an individual Spend Money or Write Cheques entry. If you like to be able to see a running list of transactions, so you don't lose track of where you're up to, then working with the registers works best. If you prefer to add a whole lot of extra detail about each transaction — splitting transactions across multiple lines or adding detailed memos — then recording individual entries works best.

2. **Start by selecting the correct bank account.**

   If you have more than one bank account, make sure you select the correct bank account for each transaction.

3. **Be careful with dates, but don't worry about entering stuff in date order.**

   Accounting software sorts everything in date order automatically, regardless of what sequence you use to record transactions.

4. **Think hard about what tax code you select.**

   Tax codes are the secret to success when working with accounting software. Instead of entering the dollar amount of GST, you enter a tax code and the software calculates GST automatically. You can also usually toggle whether you enter amounts including GST, or excluding GST.

5. **If you pay someone regularly, set up a 'record' for them.**

   In this context, a *record* is a new supplier listing. One neat thing about accounting software (when compared to handwritten books or spreadsheets) is that if you record a name against a transaction and set up this name in the supplier list (or whatever this list is called in your accounting software), then you can generate transaction reports based on this supplier name.

6. **Think about what other information could be useful from a business management perspective.**

   A neat thing about accounting software is that you can record a lot of extra information about each transaction, coding transactions according to individual projects, locations, salespeople and much more. Can you record additional info about each transaction that may help this business succeed?

7. **Decide whether to process this transaction electronically.**

   With most accounting software, you can choose whether to create a bank payments file which you then open using your internet banking software, ready to pay the supplier. With some software, you can even process payments from within the accounting software itself. (See the sidebar 'Traditional bookkeeping turned on its head' for more details.)

Nitpicking over Petty Cash

You can find as many different ways to deal with petty cash as there are to make bolognaise sauce. But a few things never change:

- ✔ Chocolate bars, roses for the beautiful girl at the train station and vet bills are not legitimate petty cash receipts.

- ✔ When someone takes petty cash from the tin and promises to come back with a receipt, they probably won't.

- ✔ When someone sticks an IOU in the petty cash tin, it means that they'd love to pay you back, but they're just not sure whether it will be this century or the next.

- ✔ No matter how finicky you are, petty cash will never, ever balance.

In the next couple of sections, I talk about two ways to deal with petty cash. The first method is best for businesses with a few employees and a petty cash tin. The second method is best for owner-operators paying expenses out of their own pockets. Take a look and see which suits you best.

Storing cash under lock and key

If a business has employees who sometimes pay for business expenses by cash, you need to set up a decent petty cash system. Here's the whole deal, from start to finish:

1. **Buy a petty cash box.**

   It's time to liberate your cash from the biscuit tin. Instead, buy a real petty cash box with a lock and key.

2. **Appoint a gatekeeper.**

   Put someone in charge of petty cash and make sure no-one else knows where the key is kept. If you're the owner of the business, this may feel a bit weird but hey, you're not allowed to raid the petty cash tin for Indian takeaways and meat pies any more. Those days are gone.

3. **Start a float between $100 and $200.**

   Write a cash cheque for a round amount (about $100) and put this cash in the tin. When you record this cheque, allocate it to an asset account called Petty Cash. If you don't already have an asset account by this name in your chart of accounts, then create one now.

4. **Every time anyone takes money out of the tin, get a receipt.**

   This is the part that requires a huge leap in psychology. Every time someone takes money from petty cash, they have to come back with a receipt. This is pretty radical. It works well if the gatekeeper hassles everyone mercilessly: No receipt, no cash next time!

   By the way, if someone doesn't have a receipt, you can't cover things up by just writing out a petty cash voucher for the missing amount. A petty cash voucher, even if you describe what the item was for, isn't a valid receipt in the eyes of an auditor who's baying for blood.

5. **When petty cash is low, sort out the receipts.**

   When petty cash funds dwindle, tip all the receipts out and sort them into piles. Write a breakdown of the receipts on the back of an envelope (for example, $35 for petrol, $25.50 for postage, $11 for coffee, $6 for toilet rolls, $17 for stationery and so on), and stuff the receipts into the envelope. Of course, if you want to list these entries using a simple spreadsheet similar to Figure 6-4, that's fine too.

6. Write a cheque to top petty cash up to the original value of the float.

Here's the brain-drain: If you're left with $4.50 in the tin and the original float was $100, write a cash cheque for $95.50. Or, if you're left with $4.50 and the original float was $200, write a cash cheque for $195.50.

7. Record the cash cheque in your payments journal, splitting it across a number of different allocation accounts.

In Figure 6-5, I select my Business Cheque account as the bank account, and select individual expense accounts as the allocation accounts. An alternative method is to select your Petty Cash account as the bank account and individual expense accounts as the allocation accounts, and then record a second transaction that has your Business Cheque account as the bank account and the Petty Cash account as the allocation account. Either method works fine.

					Staff Amenities	Staff Amenities		
	Amount	Cleaning	Petrol	Postage	with GST	no GST	Stationery	
Petty Cash Summary October 12								
1/02/2010	18.00		18.00					
2/02/2010	11.00			11.00				
5/02/2010	17.00		17.00					
5/02/2010	10.50						10.50	
6/02/2010	7.90			7.90				
6/02/2010	6.60			6.60				
6/02/2010	6.50						6.50	
10/02/2010	11.00					11.00		
12/02/2010	6.00				6.00			
	94.50	-	35.00	25.50	6.00	11.00	17.00	

Figure 6-4: You can use a spreadsheet to list petty cash receipts.

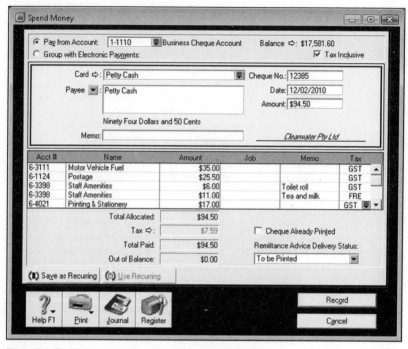

Figure 6-5: Recording expenditure from the petty cash tin.

Robbing Peter to pay Paul

Many small businesses are too small to do the whole deal with petty cash tins. Instead, owner-operators tend to pay for small business expenses using cash from their own pocket, ending up with a wallet stuffed full of dog-eared receipts. Here's my sure-fire method for recording these expenses.

1. **Every month or so, go on a mad Mintie hunt for receipts.**

   If you're the business owner reading this book, dig through your pockets, tip out your wallet, look under the seats of your car. If you're a bookkeeper, hassle your employer/client to find every receipt they can lay their hands on.

The boat that leaked

I remember my first bookkeeping job, at a busy office with a lot of people coming and going. Petty cash used to go out the door at a rate of a couple of hundred dollars per week, with rarely a receipt in return. This went on for months until finally, the accountant asked me to pull things into line.

A sweet smile, carefully worded requests and a memo sent to all staff did me no good at all. I'd come into work in the morning and find that the tin was bare (the owner's fine dining habit, I suspect). I'd top up the tin but by the afternoon any number of employees came to cadge cash, offering only a ragged IOU. in exchange. I'd write up the petty cash at the end of the week and roll

my eyes in horror. Even the receipts I did have were often dubious. I agonised — could I really justify two bottles of Moet champagne as a Staff Amenities expense? (Maybe if some of that champagne had come my way I would have been more chilled about the whole scenario.)

And so I found my inner bitch (haven't lost it yet, by the way). No IOUs anymore. No cash without a receipt first. No cash if the receipt was for meat pies and beer. Oh yes, and a new tin with a new key that only I had access to.

The result? A petty cash tin that finally balanced, and a hardened glint to my baby blue eyes.

2. **Clear a patch on your desk and sort the receipts into categories.**

   One pile for stationery, one pile for computer supplies, one pile for postage and so on. (Remember, at this point you only want receipts for things paid for by cash; put receipts for things paid for by cheque, EFTPOS or credit card in a separate pile.)

3. **Use a calculator to add up the total value of each pile, writing these totals down on the front of an empty envelope.**

   You end up with an envelope that reads something like:

   Total stationery receipts = $15.00

   Total postage receipts = $45.50

   Of course, if you want to type these entries into a simple spreadsheet similar to Figure 6-4, that's fine too.

4. Add up the total value of all petty cash receipts and write this total on the front of the envelope.

Alternatively, print your spreadsheet summary and staple it to the front of the envelope.

5. Stuff the receipts into the envelope and close it up.

6. Record a journal entry that debits each expense and credits Owner's Drawings.

You can see a typical general journal in Figure 6-6. In this journal, I debit three expense accounts (Motor Vehicle Fuel, Printing & Stationery, and Postage) and credit the Owner's Drawings account.

The method I explain here, recording a journal entry that credits drawings and debits expenses, is only appropriate for sole traders or partnerships. If you are doing the books for a company, then personal spending by directors or shareholders needs to be allocated against a Directors' Loan liability account.

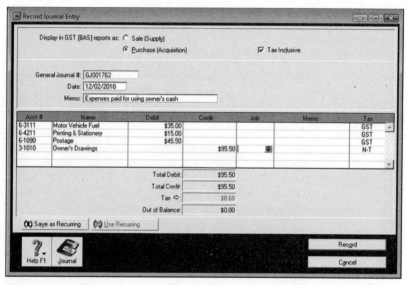

Figure 6-6: Recording a journal entry for petty cash expenses paid using owner's cash.

Choosing Allocation Accounts

Whether you do your books by hand, with a spreadsheet or
using accounting software, the real skill of bookkeeping (aside
from accuracy) is knowing what account to select when you
allocate expenses.

In Chapter 2, I talk about setting up your chart of accounts and
customising this chart to suit your business. I can't provide you
with hard-and-fast rules about what expense accounts to use
when allocating transactions because every business is unique,
but in Table 6-1, I point out the hairy bits which trap many a
novice bookkeeper.

Note: In Table 6-1, you can assume that the suggested account is
an expense account unless I specify otherwise.

Table 6-1	Matchmaking Payments and Accounts	
Type of Expense or Payment	*Comments*	*Use This Account*
Bank charges	Regular bank charges go to Bank Fees, and bank charges for merchant facilities (credit cards) go to Merchant Fees. Interest goes to Interest Expense.	Bank Fees Interest Expense Merchant Fees
Coffee, biscuits, tea, toilet rolls	The essentials for happy employees go into an account called Staff Amenities.	Staff Amenities
Government charges	Company return lodgements go to Filing Fees, licence renewals go to Licence Fees and stamp duty on insurance goes to Insurance Expense.	Filing Fees Licence Fees Insurance Expense

(continued)

Table 6-1 *(continued)*

Type of Expense or Payment	Comments	Use This Account
Hire purchase/leases	A hire purchase is a different beastie to a lease. Ask your accountant if you're not sure what you have.	Hire Purchase (liability) Lease Expense
Miscellaneous expenses	Avoid accounts such as Sundry Expense or Miscellaneous Expense. Instead, create a new account or use an existing account which is a close match.	Office Supplies Repairs & Maintenance Staff Amenities
Motor vehicle expenses	If you have more than one vehicle and these vehicles are used for both personal and business, create separate accounts for each motor vehicle.	Motor Vehicle Fuel Motor Vehicle Insurance Motor Vehicle Repairs
New equipment	If new equipment goes over a certain dollar value (this value depends on the type and size of the business), allocate this purchase to an asset account, not an expense. If you're not sure what value this threshold is, consult your accountant.	Furniture & Fittings (asset) Plant & Equipment (asset) Asset Pool (asset)
Office repairs	If a repair is minor, allocate to Repairs & Maintenance. If a repair counts as an improvement (a new verandah or skylight, for example) it is probably an asset. Ask your accountant if you're not sure.	Repairs & Maintenance Leasehold Improvements (asset) Building Improvements (asset)

Type of Expense or Payment	Comments	Use This Account
Personal spending (sole trader or partnership)	Always be careful to separate personal spending from business spending.	Personal Drawings (equity account)
Personal spending (director or shareholder of a company)	A company director or shareholder can only use company funds for personal purposes if they take these funds in the form of wages or directors' fees or as a debit against a Directors' or Shareholders' Loan account.	Directors' Loan (liability account) Directors' Fees Wages Expense
Stock purchases	If you track inventory costs and stock levels, allocate new purchases to an account called Inventory. Otherwise, allocate stock purchases to a Purchases account.	Inventory Purchases (cost of sales account)
Subcontractors	Never muddle subbies and employees and keep subbie payments entirely separate from wages.	Subcontractor Expense
Superannuation	If you use payroll software, allocate super payments to Superannuation Payable. Otherwise, allocate to Superannuation Expense.	Superannuation Payable (liability) Superannuation Expense
Taxes	Every bookkeeper's nightmare! Be careful where you allocate tax payments and remember that the only tax payments that ever get coded as an expense are Fringe Benefits Tax and Land Tax.	Provision for Company Tax (liability) Fringe Benefits Tax (expense) GST Collected/Paid (liability) PAYG Payable (liability) Personal Drawings (Tax) (equity)

(continued)

Table 6-1 *(continued)*

Type of Expense or Payment	Comments	Use This Account
Tools	If new tools are over a certain dollar value (ask your accountant what threshold applies), then allocate this purchase to an asset account, not an expense.	Plant & Equipment (asset) Replacement Tools (expense)
Travel	Keep local travel separate from overseas travel (and remember that overseas travel doesn't have any GST on it).	Travel Expense Domestic Travel Expense Overseas
Wages	Remember that your wages account should report on gross wages, not net wages.	Wages Expense

Personally speaking

One of the trickier tasks a bookkeeper faces is slicing and dicing expenses that are part-personal and part-business. For example, I work from my office at home, and my electricity bill is a mix of business and personal expense.

The rules for splitting home and business expenses can be tricky. The simplest approach for you, as a bookkeeper, is to speak to the company accountant and find out what the rules are and what percentage personal use you need to apply. Diarise this conversation, making a specific note of what the accountant recommends you do. With this understanding in place, split each transaction at the time that you record it. For example, I pay my electricity bill out of my business account, and at the time I record the transaction in my accounting software, I allocate 30 per cent to business expense and the remainder to personal.

Recording Purchases, Not Just Payments

In Chapter 3, I explain how you can do accounts on a cash basis or an accrual basis. So far in this chapter, I've assumed that you're doing books on a cash basis: When payments are made, you record these payments in your accounts.

With accrual accounting, you recognise expenses at the time you receive a bill from a supplier, regardless of when you pay this bill. Later, when you pay this bill, you record the payment as a second transaction.

As a bookkeeper, you need to evaluate whether you actually should record supplier bills as soon as you receive them, or whether it is going to work fine simply to record supplier bills when they get paid.

I can't make this decision for you, but I can explain the upsides and downsides of doing your books on an accrual basis.

Some benefits of accrual-basis accounting for purchases include:

- ✔ You can claim GST on bills that you've received, but haven't paid for yet. (This only applies if you report for GST on an accrual basis).

- ✔ At the click of a button, you can see exactly how much you owe suppliers.

- ✔ You can easily see whether accounts are overdue (and by how much) before things get out of hand.

- ✔ You can see what bills you have to pay when and plan your cashflow better.

- ✔ Your monthly Profit & Loss reports are more accurate, because expenses show up in the month to which they belong, rather than showing up in the month that you pay them.

- ✔ When you're ready to pay suppliers, processing payments is quick, easy and efficient.

The downsides of accrual-basis accounting for purchases are:

- ✔ Every supplier invoice involves two entries instead of one. That's because you first record the supplier bill as a purchase, and then later you record the supplier payment, instead of recording the bill and payment as one transaction in your cash payments journal.

- ✔ Accrual accounting can be tricky to get your head around, especially if you're new to bookkeeping.

If you use your accounting software to keep tabs on inventory costs and inventory levels, then you automatically need to enter supplier bills as soon as you receive stock. You may even want to enter supplier bills before you receive stock, in the form of purchase orders that you can then fax or email to the supplier.

In this situation, using accrual accounting for keeping track of purchases is a no-brainer, because you need to enter supplier bills as soon as you receive them so that your stock levels and costs are accurate and up to date.

I explain more about the debits and credits behind accrual accounting, and provide more in-depth info about tracking outstanding supplier accounts in *Bookkeeping For Dummies*, Australian & New Zealand edition.

Chapter 7

Recording Receipts and Sales

● ●

In This Chapter

▶ Recording sales and customer payments — different strokes for different folks

▶ Doing the books for other kinds of income

▶ Staying wise to who owes you money

● ●

*E*veryone loves to receive money. I know I do. And so the part of bookkeeping where you get to catalogue sales and match up customer payments is kind of fun.

As a bookkeeper, keeping tabs on how much customers owe is life-and-death stuff. If a business doesn't chase customers for overdue accounts or extends too much credit without realising, the consequences can get pretty dire. As a bookkeeper, your job is to make sure the books are accurate and up to date, and to keep on the back of recalcitrant payers.

In this chapter, I explain how to keep a simple cash receipts register, and I also explain how to record customer invoices, match payments against invoices, and record other kinds of income, such as bank interest or capital contributions. I also show no fear and delve into the lonely corridors of customer credits and discounts, refunds and rebates, and last but not least, the sad act of writing off bad debts.

Tailoring for the Perfect Fit

A bookkeeper can keep track of income in many different ways. What works best depends on the size of the business that you're doing books for, your budget and what you're most familiar with. Here are just a few possible approaches:

✔ If you prefer to do books by hand, the simplest method is to write up a receipts journal that lists all money received in date order, and includes columns for the date, customer name, amount, payment method and GST. See 'Writing up sales by hand' later in this chapter for more details.

✔ You can create a receipts journal in the same way using a spreadsheet, although you may prefer to combine payments and receipts on a single worksheet. See 'Working up a sweat with spreadsheets' later in this chapter for more details.

✔ You can use accounting software not only to record customer payments, but also to generate sales invoices. See 'Recording sales using accounting software' and 'Recording customer payments using accounting software' later in this chapter for more details.

The principles of bookkeeping stay constant whatever method you use, and in this chapter I don't attempt to cast judgement about the pros and cons of handwritten books versus spreadsheets, or spreadsheets versus accounting software. I leave that job to Chapter 4. Instead I explore all three methods, outlining a strategy for each one.

I don't give detailed step-by-step guides when explaining how to perform tasks using accounting software because this kind of instruction depends on the software you're using. However, if you need more specific info for either MYOB or QuickBooks software, check out the companion titles *MYOB Software For Dummies* and *QuickBooks QB^i For Dummies*, both written by yours truly and published by Wiley Australia.

Writing up sales by hand

In Figure 7-1 you can see a typical handwritten *receipts journal*, a term that bookkeepers use to describe a journal that records all transactions relating to business income. This journal lists transactions in date order, showing the amount, including GST, the payment method, the amount of tax and the net value of each sale.

You can probably make a stab at doing a receipts journal just by buying a ledger book from the newsagent and copying this format, but I'll chuck a few comments into the mix to help you along:

1. **List all transactions in date order.**

   Work directly from your bank statement, listing each deposit on a separate line. Remember to include miscellaneous income such as bank interest.

2. **Show GST in a separate column.**

   Figure 7-1 shows a separate column for GST.

3. **Write the net value of each receipt in the relevant income column.**

   By net, I mean the value before GST. For example, the first line of Figure 7-1 shows daily banking of $1,890. I write $1,890 in the Amount column, $171.82 in the GST column and $1718.18 in the Sales column. On the second line, I write $12 in the Amount column, nothing in the GST column and $12 in the Bank Interest column. If you make any GST-free sales, create an additional column for these sales.

Receipts Journal

Date	Description	Amount	Eftpos	Cheque	Cash	GST	Sales	Bank Interest	Other
2/10/2010	Daily banking	1,890.00	600.00	150.00	1,140.00	171.82	1,718.18		
2/10/2010	Interest	12.00			12.00	-		12.00	
3/10/2010	Daily banking	750.00	320.00	-	430.00	68.18	681.82		
4/10/2010	Daily banking	1,455.00	1,020.00	90.00	345.00	132.27	1,322.73		
4/10/2010	Proceeds from bank loan	10,000.00			10,000.00	-			10,000.00
5/10/2010	Daily banking	990.00	627.00	72.00	291.00	90.00	900.00		
6/10/2010	Daily banking	1,020.00	880.00	20.00	120.00	92.73	927.27		
	Totals	16,117.00	3,447.00	332.00	12,338.00	555.00	5,550.00	12.00	10,000.00
	Check Sum!				16,117.00				16,117.00

Figure 7-1: A typical handwritten receipts journal.

4. **Add any transactions where you didn't bank the cash.**

   If you sometimes receive cash and don't bank it, show these sales in a separate column called 'Cash Not Banked' and change the name of the 'Cash' column to become 'Cash Banked'.

5. **Double-check that the bank statement accurately reflects 'source' records such as deposit books and EFTPOS merchant totals.**

   Get the deposit book and make sure that for every page in the deposit book, a matching amount shows up on the bank statement (this process guards against money going missing or getting banked into the wrong bank account, or the bank making mistakes). Similarly, match daily EFTPOS merchant totals against daily deposits on the bank statement.

Sales journals, subsidiary ledgers and other scary stuff

These days, most people who rely on handwritten books only do so because their record-keeping needs are very simple. However, before accounting software became par for the course, even large businesses used hand-written books. Their systems were more complex, particularly when accounting for sales made on credit.

If you do books by hand and want to track goods sold on credit, you need to maintain not only a cash receipts journal, but also a *sales journal* (a journal that lists the value of every sale made) and a set of individual ledgers for each customer (also sometimes called an *accounts*

receivable ledger). Every time you make a sale, you write it up in both the sales journal and the individual customer ledger. Every time you receive a payment, you write it up in both the receipts journal and the individual customer ledger.

I don't devote precious pages of this *For Dummies* guide to explaining this method. Instead, I recommend that if you want to keep track of who's paid and who hasn't, you either purchase accounting software, or you use a simple system such as a ring binder folder where you store a copy of every invoice sent, marking off each invoice as you receive payment.

6. **Grab your calculator and total each column.**

7. **Double-check that the totals match.**

   Add up the total of the GST column and all the columns
   to the right of that column, and write this total on the
   bottom line in the far-right column (in Figure 7-1, this
   total equals $16,117). Compare this total to the total
   of the Amount column. The two figures should match!
   In addition, add up the total of each payment method
   column (in Figure 7-1, I add up the columns for EFTPOS,
   cheque and cash). I can sleep easy tonight, knowing that
   this grand total also equals $16,117.

Working up a sweat with spreadsheets

In Chapter 6, I talk about writing up payments and receipts using
a spreadsheet; and in Figure 6-2, I show a journal with both types
of transactions, along with a column that tracks the running
balance. I favour this method for small businesses with a limited
number of payments and receipts.

However, if you do a lot of income analysis, or if you have a
mixture of taxable and non-taxable sales, you may prefer to
mimic traditional bookkeeping and maintain one spreadsheet for
cash payments and another spreadsheet for cash receipts.

In Figure 7-2, you can see a cash receipts spreadsheet that's
pretty much the exact mirror of the handwritten transactions
in Figure 7-1. The beauty of spreadsheets is that they do all
the adding automatically, so long as you insert a few simple
formulas. In Figure 7-2, I've changed the view settings so you can
see what formulas I've used.

By the way, I find that spreadsheets work well for recording
customer receipts but aren't ideal for tracking how much
customers owe you. However, a small owner-operated
business can get away with generating invoices using a word
processor, filing invoice copies in a folder and marking each
invoice when payment is received. Alternatively, you can keep
things real simple, writing invoices by hand using a carbon-copy
invoice book and marking each invoice copy when you receive
payment.

	Figure 0902 [Compatibility Mode] - Microsoft Excel										
Home	Insert	Page Layout	Formulas	Data	Review	View					

M18

	B	C	D	E	F	G	H	I	J	K	L	M
1	**Receipts Journal**											
3	Date	Description of transaction	Amount	Eftpos	Cheque	Cash	Tax?		GST		Sales	Bank Interest
6	40453	Daily banking	1890	600	150	=D6-E6-F6	Yes	=IF(I6="No",0,D6/11)			=D6-J6	
7	40453	Interest	12			=D7-E7-F7	No	=IF(I7="No",0,D7/11)				=D7
8	40454	Daily banking	750	320	0	=D8-E8-F8	Yes	=IF(I8="No",0,D8/11)			=D8-J8	
9	40455	Daily banking	1455	1020	90	=D9-E9-F9	Yes	=IF(I9="No",0,D9/11)			=D9-J9	
10	40455	Proceeds from bank loan	10000			=D10-E10-F10	No	=IF(I10="No",0,D10/11)				
11	40456	Daily banking	990	627	72	=D11-E11-F11	Yes	=IF(I11="No",0,D11/11)			=D11-J11	
12	40457	Daily banking	1020	880	20	=D12-E12-F12	Yes	=IF(I12="No",0,D12/11)			=D12-J12	
13												
14		Totals	=SUM(D6:D12)	=SUM(E6:E12)	=SUM(F6:F12)	=SUM(G6:G12)			=SUM(J6:J12)		=SUM(L6:L12)	=SUM(M6:M12)
15												
16		Check Sum!				=E14+F14+G14						

Payments Journal   Receipts Journal

Ready   100%

Figure 7-2: Using formulas in spreadsheets makes doing your books much quicker.

Recording sales using accounting software

When you record income from customers using accounting software, you don't simply record the receipt of money. Instead, you use the accounting software to first record the sale and then later, when you receive money from the customer, to record the payment.

I explain in Chapter 3 the difference between cash and accrual accounting. When you beaver away using a receipts journal — which is what I talk about in the earlier sections 'Writing up sales by hand' and 'Working up a sweat with spreadsheets' — you work on a cash basis. On the other hand, when you record sales and then payments — which is what happens when you use accounting software — you work on an accrual basis.

Although the precise details of how to record sales using accounting software vary, depending on what software you use, here are some general tips to bear in mind:

- **Cash or credit?** Some accounting software differentiates between cash sales and sales on credit, using different screens for each type of sale.

- **How is GST calculated?** With accounting software, instead of entering the dollar amount of GST, you usually enter a tax code and the software calculates GST automatically. For this reason, setting up tax codes properly is absolutely vital (refer to Chapter 5 for more about this topic). Remember that most software lets you toggle between entering transactions inclusive, or exclusive, of GST.

✔ **Is it best to set up items, even for services?** Most accounting software lets you set up 'items' for billing. Items can be for services, not just products. I often set up things such as hourly rates as individual 'items', making for swift and accurate billing. You can see how this works in Figure 7-3.

✔ **What account do you want to allocate this sale to?** I like to provide business owners with as much information about their business performance as possible, and so I like to split income into a few different categories, creating a different account for each one. For example, I split my own income into consulting income, freelance writing income and royalty income.

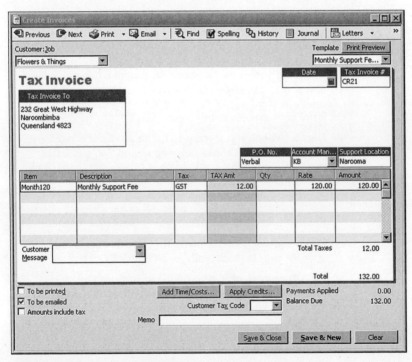

Figure 7-3: Entering a sale in QuickBooks.

✔ **What's the best layout?** Spend time thinking about how you want your invoice to look, and take care to customise the layout (also sometimes called 'forms' or 'templates'). Sure, your main responsibility is probably to produce a clean set of books, but the invoices that customers receive should look smart and professional.

✔ **What other info do you want to include?** The neat thing about accounting software is that you can record a lot of extra information about each transaction, coding transactions according to individual projects, locations, salespeople, shipping details or promised delivery date. Ask yourself, what additional info could you record about each sale that may be useful for this business?

Recording customer payments using accounting software

I can't be that specific about how to record customer payments using accounting software because I don't know what software you're using, but I can provide a few general tips:

✔ **Cultivate your inner pedant:** Be careful when recording dates. If you're imprecise about the date, you make life much harder for yourself when it comes to reconciling bank accounts later on.

✔ **Decide whether you want to batch payments together:** You can usually choose between depositing customer payments into your bank account or grouping customer payments in an undeposited funds account. If you bank several payments in a batch each day, I recommend you use an undeposited funds account; otherwise, simply select the bank account into which you'll bank this payment.

✔ **File remittance advices:** When customers send remittance advices, file them carefully in date order.

✔ **Pick the payment method with precision:** The method a customer chooses to pay affects when the money appears in your account. For example, EFTPOS, Visa and MasterCard transactions usually appear as a single batch the day after the transaction; cheques appear in your bank account when you slog up to the bank to deposit them; and cash may get banked or it may get spent. Diners Club and American Express appear in separate batches some days later.

✔ **Play the matchmaking game with care:** When you record a customer payment, you usually have to match this payment against specific invoices. Sounds easy, but sometimes a customer overpays, underpays or pays a recent invoice and forgets an older one. Sometimes the customer deducts a credit that they think you owe them, or sometimes a customer pays a totally weird amount altogether. As a bookkeeper extraordinaire, try to figure out exactly what the customer is paying for and if they make a mistake, waste no time communicating with the customer to get the problem fixed.

✔ **Stay alert for customer credits:** With most accounting software, applying credits against invoices is a manual (rather than an automatic) process. Figure out the inner workings of the software and get on top of credits ... before they get on top of you.

Debits and credits unplugged

Want to understand the debits and credits behind cash sales and credit sales? Here goes:

Imagine I make a cash sale for $100, with $10 GST. The journal behind this transaction is:

	Debit	Credit
Cash at Bank	$110.00	
GST Collected		$10.00
Income from Sales		$100.00

Now imagine I make a credit sale for $100, with $10 GST. The journal behind this transaction is:

	Debit	Credit
Accounts Receivable	$110.00	
GST Collected		$10.00
Income from Sales		$100.00

And then when the payment is made, the journal looks like this:

	Debit	Credit
Cash at Bank	$110.00	
Accounts Receivable		$110.00

Bookkeeping for Other Kinds of Income

Sometimes you receive money from sources other than your customers. Perhaps you receive a refund from a cancelled insurance policy, the bank pays you some interest or you receive a loan from Great-Aunt Thelma. You still have to record this money in your books; the burning question is, how?

Recording miscellaneous receipts

If you do books by hand, you record miscellaneous receipts in your receipts journal, mixed up with regular income from sales. You can see how this works in Figure 7-1, where I record not only sales receipts in my journal, but bank interest and a new bank loan also.

The same principle goes for a spreadsheet: You record miscellaneous receipts in the same way as you record any other income. Just be careful that you separate these receipts from regular sales using a different column, adding a comments column if necessary.

With accounting software, things get a little different. With most software you record sales in a specific menu, and customer payments in another menu that's designed specifically for matching up payments against invoices. When it comes to miscellaneous receipts, you don't usually record these as sales, but instead as a bank deposit or supplier refund.

For example, in MYOB software, you record miscellaneous receipts in the Receive Money window in the Banking command centre (whereas you record customer payments in the Receive Payments window in the Sales command centre). Similarly, with QuickBooks, the method depends on the kind of receipt: You record supplier refunds using supplier credit notes; interest is entered via cash receipts; and you record new loans via the Record Deposits menu.

Dazzling everyone with your brilliance

Whether you do your books by hand, with a spreadsheet or using accounting software, what transforms an ordinary bookkeeper into a killer bookkeeper (asides from accuracy) is the ability to choose the correct account for each transaction.

In Chapter 2, I talk about setting up your chart of accounts and customising this chart to suit your business. I can't provide you with hard-and-fast rules about what income accounts to use when allocating transactions because every business is unique, but in Table 7-1, I point out the tricky transactions which catch many a bookkeeper unaware.

Table 7-1	Matchmaking Receipts and Accounts	
Type of Income Payment	*Comments*	*Use This Account*
Regular sales	For most businesses, I recommend you allocate sales into a few different categories, depending on your business.	Income from Service Sales; Income from Product Sales and so on
Bank interest	Always distinguish between interest income (money the bank gives you) and interest expense (money you pay the bank).	Interest Income
Dividends	Remember to account for any imputation credits on dividends.	Dividend Income
Insurance claims	Be sure to check the GST status of any payments received from insurance claims.	Insurance Recovery
Receipt of bank loans	Whatever you do, don't allocate money coming in from a bank loan to income. It's not! Create a new liability account for each new bank loan.	Loan from Bank (liability account)

(continued)

Table 7-1 *(continued)*

Type of Income Payment	Comments	Use This Account
Receipt of personal funds (sole trader or partnership)	For small amounts, allocate as a credit to the Drawings account. For large amounts, create a new equity account called Owner's Contributions or Partner's Contributions.	Owner's Drawings Partner's Drawings Owner's Contributions Partner's Contributions
Receipt of personal funds (via a company director or shareholder)	Allocate to a Directors' Loan account.	Directors' Loan (liability account)
Rental income	Unless the core focus of a business concerns property investment, separate rental income from regular income so that the income doesn't affect gross profit.	Rental Income
Sale of equipment or motor vehicles	Ask the company accountant how best to record this transaction and check the GST status of this income.	Sale of Assets Profit & Loss on Asset Disposal
Supplier refunds	Allocate the supplier refund against whatever expense account you allocated the original payment to.	Purchases Insurance Expense Telephone Expense
Tax refunds	For sole traders or partnerships, allocate to a Drawings account. For companies, allocate to Provision for Company Tax.	Owner's Drawings Partner's Drawings Provision for Company Tax

If you get a bank loan, that's not income. If your secret lover has a heart attack and leaves you everything in the final will, that's not income. If you deposit your life's savings into your new entrepreneurial venture exporting sheep to New Zealand (oh no, please don't), that's not income. Income is only income when you earn it. Simple as that.

Keeping Track of Who Owes You What

One of the most important parts of a bookkeeper's job is to keep track of how much customers owe the business. I talk more about the art of debt collection in Chapter 10, but in this chapter, I focus on how to generate a report showing how much customers owe you.

All accounting software includes as standard an *Aged Receivables report*, a report that lists how much each customer owes, sorted in columns according to how old the debt is. Figure 7-4 shows a typical report.

Keep this report sweet by taking a few tips on board:

✔ As your business grows, review your Aged Receivables report every week. Make sure that the percentage of accounts that are overdue doesn't increase month after month, and don't wait until you're already strapped for cash before asking customers to cough up.

✔ As a conscientious bookkeeper, if amounts appear on this report that you don't understand — for example, a customer shows as owing money but you're positive they paid — then figure out why the report is wrong, and fix it!

✔ With most software, you can double-click on any amount to see the individual invoices that make up a customer's debt, or you can print a detailed Aged Receivables report that lists every invoice outstanding, sorted by customer.

✔ The older an account is, the less likely the customer is to pay. So beware!

✔ If you bill customers weekly or fortnightly, you're best to see whether you can modify this report to specify either 7 or 14 days as the number of days per ageing period.

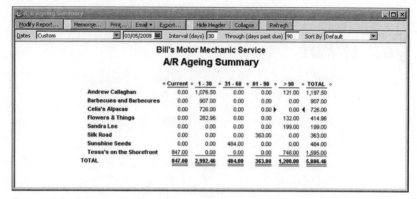

Figure 7-4: An Aged Receivables report shows how much customers owe you.

Chapter 8

Reconciling Accounts

• •

In This Chapter

▶ Calculating your opening bank balance

▶ Getting your first bank reconciliation off the runway

▶ Employing tricks of the trade when all seems lost

• •

*W*hen you reconcile a bank account, you compare the transactions in your set of accounts to those on the corresponding bank statement. You tick these entries off one by one and check that you and your bank agree, down to the very last cent.

Reconciling bank accounts isn't some arcane activity invented by masochistic bean counters. Rather, reconciling accounts is the only sure-fire way to identify if you have made any mistakes, such as a payment entered as $900 instead of $90, a deposit entered twice or missing bank fees.

The good news is that reconciling bank accounts is surprisingly quick and easy and, although you may find this hard to believe, can even be rather satisfying in a weird, nerdish kind of way. (I'm not really a boring person. Just sometimes, I get excited over boring things. Spot the difference . . .)

Getting Started

Did you ever see that old movie *A Christmas Carol*, based on the book by Charles Dickens? The beleaguered accounts clerk Bob Cratchit, under pressure from his heartless employer Ebenezer Scrooge, spends Christmas Eve completing the final bank reconciliation for his employer. Only when this reconciliation is complete is he permitted to go home for Christmas dinner with his family.

I hope that you're never going to spend Christmas Eve getting your bank account to reconcile. Instead, use my easy step-by-step approach to the gentle art of reconciliation, and make sure you spend every festive occasion eating, drinking and being merry.

Deciding what bank accounts to reconcile

Most businesses have a lot of bank accounts, from savings accounts and term deposits, to credit cards and loans. A conscientious bookkeeper — and I hope that's what you are — knows to reconcile all of these accounts. However, if you're not conscientious — maybe you're the owner of the business and you're happy for your accountant to pick up after you — I suggest you slot bank reconciliations into three categories:

- ✔ **Accounts you have to reconcile:** As a bare minimum, always reconcile the main business bank account. Unless you do this, neither you nor anyone else can rely on any financial reports.

- ✔ **Accounts to reconcile if you have time:** It's a good idea to reconcile all credit card, savings and PayPal accounts, as well as the business bank account.

- ✔ **Accounts to reconcile if you're feeling conscientious:** Ideally, reconcile all loan accounts as well. Loan accounts can be tricky, because you have to split up interest and principal on each loan repayment.

Calculating your true bank balance

Unless you're a new business with a nil opening balance in your bank account, the first time you reconcile a bank account, you need to calculate what the *true balance* of this account is. By true balance (also sometimes referred to as *cashbook balance*), I mean the bank statement balance adjusted for any uncleared withdrawals or deposits. For example, maybe my bank statement says I have $1,500 in my account. However, I know that I just wrote a cheque for $200 to puppy pre-school (a tax deduction for sure, this ball of fluff is one fierce guard dog), and that this cheque hasn't cleared yet. I also accepted a credit card payment from a customer for $1,200 that hasn't shown up in my account yet. My true bank balance is actually $2,500 (that's $1,500 less $200 plus $1,200).

Being a nerdy kind of gal, I like to draw up a wee report showing how I calculate this true balance, similar to Figure 8-1. (I typed this report in a word processor, but, of course, you can write this report just fine by hand.) The process is a tad technical, but don't stress out. Here's what to do:

1. **Look up the opening balance on the bank statement.**

    For example, if you're starting your books from 1 July 2010, dig out the July bank statement. Write down the statement balance as at this date.

2. **List all uncleared withdrawals as at your starting date and write down the total amount.**

    By *uncleared*, I mean any cheques written before this date which haven't been presented yet.

3. **List all uncleared deposits as at your starting date and write down the total amount.**

    Look at the deposit book for this period to see if there are any deposits that didn't clear immediately. An example may be a deposit dated 30 June that didn't clear through the bank account until 1 July, or EFTPOS payments received from customers on 30 June that didn't appear on the bank statement until 1 July.

4. **Work out what the true bank account balance was at your starting date.**

    The *true* bank account balance is what you would have in your account if all uncleared payments and deposits cleared immediately. In other words, the true bank balance is the amount you wrote down in Step 1 (the balance from your bank statement), less the amount you wrote down in Step 2 (total uncleared payments), plus the amount you wrote down in Step 3 (total uncleared deposits).

5. **Write this information neatly as a report.**

    See Figure 8-1 for a most glamorous and elegant example.

Bank Reconciliation for Business Account 30 June	
Balance as per bank statement	$ 1,500.00
Less: Uncleared cheques	
00471	$ 200.00
Subtotal	$ 1,300.00
Add: Uncleared deposits	$ 1,200.00
Cashbook Balance	$ 2,500.00

Figure 8-1: A reconciliation report showing my true bank balance.

Recording your opening bank balance using accounting software

If you're using accounting software, and you've already calculated your true bank balance (if not, refer to the section earlier called 'Calculating your true bank balance'), then you're ready to set up your first bank reconciliation. Here's my neat 1-2-3 approach:

1. **In your chart of accounts, make sure you not only have an account for your bank account, but also create a new account called Uncleared Transactions.**

   This account sits immediately below your bank account in your chart of accounts.

2. **Enter the opening bank statement balance as the opening balance for your bank account.**

   The mechanics vary, but any accounting software provides a spot for you to enter opening balances. As the opening balance for your bank account, enter the balance as per the bank statement. (In the example from Figure 8-1, I enter $1,500 as the opening balance for my bank account.)

3. **Enter the combined balance of uncleared transactions as the opening balance of your Uncleared Transactions account.**

Using the example in Figure 8-1 again, the combined balance of uncleared transactions is $1,000 (a $200 uncleared cheque, which is a minus amount, plus a $1,200 uncleared deposit).

All done? With opening balances for your bank account entered, you're ready to reconcile your bank account (see 'Reconciling accounts using software' later in this chapter for details). When the uncleared cheques or deposits eventually appear on your bank statement, simply record a transaction that transfers the amount out of your uncleared transactions account and into your regular bank account, similar to Figure 8-2.

When all uncleared transactions finally appear on your bank statement and you reconcile these transactions, your Uncleared Transactions account returns to a zero balance. Simple as pie.

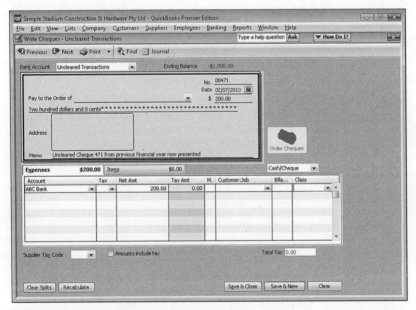

Figure 8-2: An account called Uncleared Transactions provides a neat way to account for uncleared transactions in your first bank reconciliation.

Doing Your First Reconciliation

Just like losing your you-know-what (and if you can't guess what
I'm talking about, I won't spell it out), the first time you reconcile
a bank account is certainly the most daunting. But like with most
things, practice makes perfect.

Reconciling accounts by hand

The main difference between reconciling a bank account by
hand, versus reconciling a bank account using accounting
software, is that when you reconcile a bank account by hand,
you usually reconcile a month's worth of transactions at a time.
(You also do a whole lot more adding up and ticking off and
general fussing around.) So pick up your fountain pen and get
ready for action:

1. **Write up every single transaction for the month.**

   Don't forget irregular transactions such as personal ATM
   withdrawals or monthly bank fees.

2. **Write your opening cashbook balance at the top of
   your Bank Reconciliation report.**

   By opening cashbook balance, I mean your true bank
   balance. (If you're unsure what your true bank balance
   is, refer to the section 'Calculating your true bank
   balance' earlier in this chapter.)

   Figure 8-3 shows the format of a typical Bank
   Reconciliation report. Your opening cashbook balance is
   the first line.

3. **Working from the bank statement, tick off every item
   listed in your receipts journal, checking amounts as
   you go.**

   In Chapter 7, I explain how to write up a receipts journal
   that lists every deposit into your bank account. With
   this complete, the aim of the game is to compare your
   receipts journal against the bank statement. Work from
   the top of the first page of your bank statement, finding
   the corresponding deposit in your receipts journal and
   ticking first the transaction in the journal, and then the
   transaction in your bank statement.

Of course, if you find you've made a mistake in your receipts journal, fix it up. Or, if you find you've missed any deposits, add them in now.

Bank Reconciliation for the month of July

Opening cashbook balance as at 1 July			$ 7,330.00
Total monthly receipts as per receipts journal			$22,000.00
Subtotal			$29,330.00
Less: Total monthly withdrawals as per payments journal			-$18,525.20
Closing cashbook balance as at 31 July			$10,804.80
Add: Uncleared cheques			
00471	$	30.00	
00501	$	85.00	
00510	$	202.50	$ 317.50
			$11,122.30
Less: Uncleared deposits			
EFTPOS deposits 30 June	$	1,200.00	$ 1,200.00
Subtotal			$ 9,922.30
Expected bank statement balance as per 31 July			$ 9,922.30
Actual bank balance as at 31 July			$ 9,922.30
Out of balance amount			$ -

Figure 8-3: Reconciling monthly accounts by hand.

4. Repeat this process for your payments journal.

Now mark off every withdrawal in your bank statement against your payments journal, again ticking both the bank statement and your journal for every transaction. (Chapter 6 explains more about writing a payments journal.)

5. Add up all receipts in your cash receipts journal.

Write this amount against total monthly receipts in your Bank Reconciliation report, as per Figure 8-3.

6. Add up all payments in your payments journal.

Write this amount against total monthly withdrawals in your Bank Reconciliation report, as per Figure 8-3.

7. **Calculate your closing cashbook balance.**

   Again, look to Figure 8-3 for how this works. Your closing cashbook balance is equal to your opening bank balance plus all receipts for the month less all withdrawals for the month.

8. **Make a list of any cheques or deposits that are uncleared.**

   Make a list of any transactions that you haven't marked off as appearing on your bank statement, as per Figure 8-3.

9. **Calculate your expected bank statement balance.**

   Your expected bank statement balance is equivalent to your closing cashbook balance plus any uncleared cheques less any uncleared deposits. Yeah, yeah. Bookkeeping is an art form, that's for sure.

10. **Either give yourself a pat on the back, or find out where you went wrong.**

   Compare your expected bank statement balance with your actual bank balance. If the two don't match, start at Step 1 and figure out where you went wrong. (Don't be sad. Without some challenge, you don't get that sweet rush of victory when things finally balance.)

Reconciling accounts with spreadsheets

You can either use a spreadsheet to mirror a set of handwritten books, with one worksheet for payments and another for receipts, or you can create a single worksheet for each bank account, listing payments and receipts in date order, with a running bank account balance down the right-hand side. (I talk more about both of these methods in chapters 6 and 7.)

If you use one worksheet for payments and another for receipts, you do a bank reconciliation using exactly the same method as if you reconcile by hand (see 'Reconciling accounts by hand' earlier in this chapter for details). Of course, you can create a bank reconciliation as part of this spreadsheet, and use formulas to do all the adding and subtracting.

If you list both receipts and payments in a single worksheet, with a running bank balance, then use this simple approach instead:

1. **Compare your bank statement against the running bank balance in the spreadsheet, line by line.**

   If the running balance differs at any point, find where you've gone wrong and fix up the mistake.

2. **Go through your chequebook — if you still have one! — and identify any uncleared cheques (cheques that have been written but that haven't been cashed yet).**

3. **Look at your merchant receipts or deposit book and identify any uncleared deposits (deposits that you've received or banked but haven't shown up on the bank statement yet).**

4. **List all uncleared cheques and deposits at the bottom of the worksheet, in the same way as you list any other withdrawals or deposits.**

   The balance of your bank account, after allowing for these uncleared transactions, is your *true bank balance*. (If you're unsure what your true bank balance is, refer to the section 'Calculating your true bank balance' earlier in this chapter.)

Reconciling accounts using software

Reconciling your bank account using accounting software is a pretty straightforward process. Take my (rather hot and sweaty) hand in yours, and let me show you the way:

1. **Enter all transactions right up to date.**

   Don't forget miscellaneous transactions such as ATM withdrawals or bank fees. Also, some software lets you import transactions straight from your bank account, rather than keying transactions one by one. If this is your bag, that's fine by me.

2. **Compare the opening bank balance of your bank statement against the opening bank balance in the reconciliation window.**

   With QuickBooks, you compare the Beginning Balance in the Begin Reconciliation window against the running balance on your bank statement. When you find the spot on your bank statement that matches your Beginning Balance, you're in luck. Start reconciling from this point onwards.

MYOB software is a similar deal. Before you mark off any transactions, compare the Calculated Statement Balance in the Reconcile Accounts window against the running balance on your bank statement.

3. **Enter the date you're going to reconcile up to.**

When you do your first bank reconciliation, don't try to reconcile a whole page at a time. Instead, work in small, bite-sized chunks of a third or half of a page.

4. **Enter the closing balance from your bank statement into the appropriate spot.**

In Figure 8-4, you can see how QuickBooks prompts me to enter an Ending Balance for the day I'm reconciling up to. I get this balance straight off my bank statement. With MYOB, I enter this balance into the New Statement Balance field at the top of the Reconcile Accounts window.

5. **Working from the bank statement, tick off every transaction.**

For every withdrawal or deposit into your bank account, click against the corresponding transaction in your accounting software.

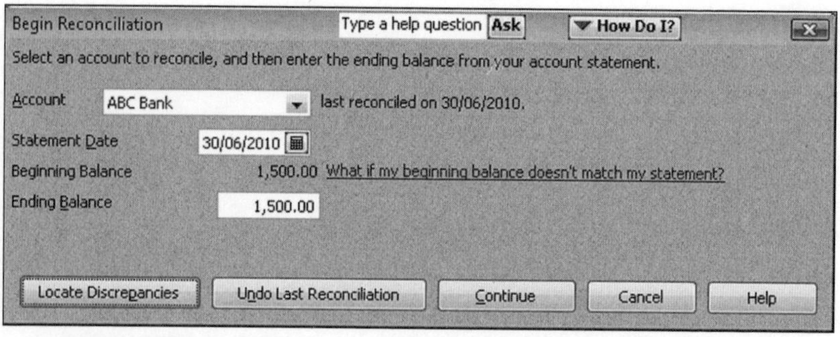

Figure 8-4: Getting ready to reconcile accounts using QuickBooks.

6. **Look to see if your bank account balances.**

   All accounting software has some way or other of letting you know whether you've got the goods, or not. QuickBooks shows a running 'Difference' amount (which in Figure 8-5, you can see is 0.00); MYOB shows a running 'Out of Balance' amount. The aim of your game, of course, is to get this figure down to zero.

7. **If you're in luck, follow the prompts to complete your reconciliation.**

   When your bank account balances, you can holler with glee. You've just completed your first bank reconciliation. If your bank account doesn't balance, don't despair. I devote whole pages of the rest of this chapter to troubleshooting tricks.

Sweeping stuff under the carpet

My high-school aged daughter does admin work for my business, and a year or so ago I decided to teach her how to reconcile my business bank account. I was in the middle of showing her how the process worked when the phone rang, and I had to dash off to see a client. I was gone most of the morning.

When I returned, she was lying happily in the hammock listening to Jack Johnson. 'How did you go?' I asked. 'Fine', she answered, 'I reconciled the last six months of your bank statements without a problem; it really doesn't seem that hard.' I approached my shiny silver iMac with a sense of trepidation that was soon justified. 'What's this entry?' I asked. 'And this one?' I highlighted a whole bunch of transactions simply labelled 'Miscellaneous', some of which were for thousands of dollars.

'Well', replied Isla. 'When I couldn't get the statement to balance, I calculated the difference, entered a transaction for that amount, marked the statement as reconciled, and then kept going. Seemed logical to me.'

I tried to explain to Isla that inventing transactions to patch up bank reconciliations is like shovelling prawn shells inside the curtain rods at your ex-lover's apartment. The problem simply festers and gets worse as time passes. After all, the idea of reconciling accounts is to find your mistakes and fix 'em up. 'What if the whole relationship was a mistake?' she asked. 'You're not getting the point', I answered. 'Never mind', she replied, and rolled over in the hammock.

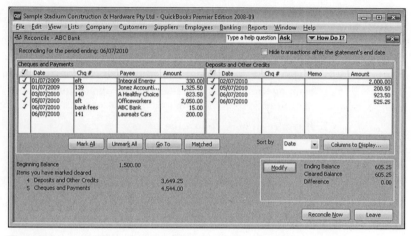

Figure 8-5: A successful bank reconciliation is a sweet thing indeed.

Troubleshooting Tricks

If your bank account doesn't balance, don't sweat. You wouldn't be human if everything went right first time around. Instead, try the following:

- **Call on your hidden powers:** How much are you out by? Does this amount ring a bell?

- **Check that your opening balance is correct:** If reconciling by hand, check that your opening balance matches the closing balance for the previous month. If reconciling using accounting software, check that the opening balance matches against the starting point on your bank statement. (With accounting software, one of the most likely reasons for a bank account not reconciling is if someone deletes or changes a transaction belonging to a previous period which has already been reconciled.)

  If your opening balance isn't correct, the solution can be quite complicated. See the sidebar 'Miss Marple does it again' for some possible tactics.

✔ **Compare the magic totals:** Somewhere on your bank statement you can usually find a summary of total debits and total credits. If you do a bank reconciliation for the same date range as this statement, you can match these totals against the totals in your reconciliation.

✔ **Divide by two:** Try dividing your out-of-balance amount by two, and look for a transaction for this amount. In other words, if you're out by $90, look for a transaction equalling $45. This trick helps locate transactions that have been entered the wrong way round (a debit instead of a credit, a payment instead of a deposit and so on).

✔ **Do the number nine trick:** If you're out by a multiple of nine, look to see if you put in two numbers back to front — for example, you entered 43 instead of 34, or 685 instead of 658. (It's a curious thing, but if you turn a number back to front and subtract your result from the original number, the difference is always exactly divisible by nine.)

✔ **Look for missing amounts:** For every line on your bank statement, make sure you tick off the corresponding transaction in your payments or receipts journal (if reconciling by hand or by a spreadsheet) or in your reconciliation window (if reconciling using software).

✔ **Make sure you're in the right spot:** Did you start off from the right spot in your bank statement? It's easy to accidentally skip a page or part of a page.

✔ **Match every amount:** Do all the amounts match? For example, don't simply compare cheque numbers on the statement against cheque numbers in your books. Make sure that the amount of every cheque is the same in both places.

✔ **Start again:** Untick everything then start again but this time reconcile just half a page of the bank statement.

✔ **Watch out when you're in the red:** If your bank account is normally in credit, but you're overdrawn, be sure to show your new balance as a minus amount.

Miss Marple does it again

If you use accounting software, one of the most challenging bookkeeping mysteries is when the opening balance of a bank account goes awry. In other words, you go to reconcile an account, but before you click off a single transaction, you can see that the opening balance doesn't match up with the bank statement that you're trying to reconcile.

I don my black lace cap and mittens (true Miss Marple attire) and start looking for clues. Is the opening balance out by an amount I recognise? (After interviewing both the butler and the maid, I search the database for the offending amount.) When did the crime occur? I use the software's 'undo reconciliation' feature, undoing the previous reconciliation, and the one before that, until I arrive at a reconciliation where the opening balance matches the bank statement for that month. Then I reconcile that month again, hopefully identifying the

perpetrator: A missing or duplicate transaction, or maybe a transaction where the amount has been altered.

If this tactic fails, or no 'undo' feature exists, I make a beeline for the audit trail. To quote Miss Marple: 'There is a great deal of wickedness in village life'. The most common cause of an incorrect opening balance is when someone deletes a transaction that they shouldn't. Like invisible fingerprints and footprints in the mud, deleted transactions are often difficult to identify, but a simple audit trail usually points to the evidence.

Unlike the real world of crime — but similar to an Agatha Christie novel — the beauty of bookkeeping is that a mistake can always be found, the crime uncovered and things put to right. All you need is a bookkeeper's stock in trade: Steely persistence and a gimlet eye.

Chapter 9

Understanding Financial Reports

*I*n this chapter, I don't explain how to generate financial reports, but instead focus on how to *understand* financial reports. I address key questions such as 'Why does this report show a profit yet there's no cash in the bank?', 'Why don't tax payments show up as an expense?' and 'How can I compare one year against another?'

Most business owners don't expect bookkeepers to understand financial reports, and many accountants are concerned that bookkeepers aren't sufficiently qualified to provide advice in this area. However, understanding the basic format of a Profit & Loss or Balance Sheet report is quite different to providing financial planning or taxation advice.

A bookkeeper who isn't afraid to produce financial reports, read them and consider the results is going to be a much better bookkeeper than someone who just does data entry and never considers the consequences. By lifting your skills this extra notch, you can be a great asset to any business (even if your value isn't listed on the Balance Sheet).

Telling the Story with Profit & Loss

A Profit & Loss report is a story, telling you how your business has fared over the past few days, months or even years. It lists sales at the top, purchases and expenses in the middle and a final profit (or loss) figure at the bottom, giving a quick and simple indication of whether a business is blooming with health or is as sick as a dog. You can see a typical Profit & Loss report in Figure 9-1.

Although most Profit & Loss reports are pretty easy to understand, don't be tempted into thinking that a profit is cause for partying and a loss is reason for a maudlin drinking bout. The important thing is to understand not only *what* the bottom line is, but *why* the business made a profit (or loss!) in the first place.

Putting income under the microscope

When you look at income in a Profit & Loss report, bear the following in mind:

✔ Income figures on a Profit & Loss report don't include GST. For this reason, the income figures on your Profit & Loss report may not match with the income figures on your sales and GST reports.

✔ Unless you specifically request a cash-based Profit & Loss report, the income on a standard Profit & Loss report shows income that the business earns, and not cash that the business receives. For example, imagine I make a single sale during March for $10,000, and no sales in the month of April, but I receive payment for my March sale on 1 April. In this scenario, my Profit & Loss reports show $10,000 income in March and zilch in April, even though April is when I received the cash.

✔ Some accountants like to separate non-trading income, such as interest or investment income, into a heading called Other Income that sits at the bottom of a Profit & Loss report.

Profit & Loss Report 1 July 2009 to 30 June 2010	Year to Date	% of Sales
Income		
Sales - Books	$ 250,200	48.0%
Sales - CDs	$ 210,600	40.4%
Sales - Gifts	$ 60,300	11.6%
Total Income	**$ 521,100**	**100.0%**
Cost of Goods Sold	$ 350,200	67.2%
Gross Profit	**$ 170,900**	**32.8%**
Expenses		
Administration Expenses		
Advertising	$ 12,240	2.3%
Bank Charges	$ 450	0.1%
Depreciation	$ 5,260	1.0%
Motor Vehicle Expenses	$ 15,800	3.0%
Postage & Stationery	$ 1,500	0.3%
Repair & Maintenance	$ 4,805	0.9%
Subscriptions	$ 850	0.2%
Occupancy Expenses		
Electricity	$ 950	0.2%
Office Rental	$ 20,101	3.9%
Payroll Expenses		
Wages & Salaries	$ 53,080	10.2%
Superannuation Expense	$ 5,430	1.0%
Workers Compensation	$ 2,420	0.5%
Total Expenses	**$ 122,886**	**23.6%**
Operating Profit	**$ 48,014**	**9.2%**
Other Income		
Interest Income	$ 456	0.1%
Net Profit/(Loss)	**$ 48,470**	**9.3%**

Figure 9-1: A typical Profit & Loss report.

Traps for the unwary

All financial reports, such as Profit & Loss and Balance Sheet reports, show figures not including GST. That's because GST isn't really income or an expense, rather GST is something that you owe to the government (when you collect GST on sales) or something you are owed from the government (when you pay GST on expenses).

Seems easy, but do keep your wits about you when comparing one report against another. For example, although a Profit & Loss report doesn't include GST, some sales reports may, depending on the software. A budget doesn't include GST, but a cashflow report usually does.

When you look at the income on a Profit & Loss report, ask yourself whether the income section of this report provides enough information. For example, do you also want to see how much income is generated from different business divisions, locations, jobs or projects?

I like to group income into at least four or five categories (something I talk about in Chapter 2), but within these categories, I often like to track the income from individual cost centres. This kind of detailed tracking is usually only practical if you use accounting software. In MYOB, the jobs and categories features provide a way to get more detail about income sources; in QuickBooks, the best approach is to use either Customer/Job details, or class tracking.

Weighing up gross profit

Cost of sales accounts are variable expenses that relate directly to sales (for more on the topic, see Chapter 2). Cost of sales accounts appear below the income accounts in a Profit & Loss report; the total of these accounts is called *cost of goods sold*.

If you deduct total cost of goods sold from total income, you arrive at a figure called *gross profit*. For example, in Figure 9-1, the total income is $521,100, the total cost of goods sold is $350,200 and the gross profit is $170,900. The percentage of gross profit against sales — 32.8 per cent in Figure 9-1 — is called the *gross profit margin*.

Be wary of miscellaneous accounts

One of my pet hates is seeing any amount on a Profit & Loss report called Miscellaneous Income, Miscellaneous Expense or General Expenses. These accounts are invariably dumping grounds for all the transactions that the bookkeeper can't find a home for.

If any of your reports include a total for Miscellaneous Income, Miscellaneous Expense or General Expenses, go do a transaction report for that account. Weed through every transaction and for each one, find a better home for it to live (and, if you're not sure where, ask the company accountant for assistance).

Oh yes, and if you're the culprit who has been dumping transactions into these accounts, stop right now! Instead, create an expense account called Suspense and allocate anything that you're not sure about into this account. At the end of every month, email a transaction report for this account to the company accountant, and ask for help allocating these transactions correctly.

As a bookkeeper, make sure you report gross profit correctly, and that the Profit & Loss report includes all variable expenses in the cost of goods sold section of the report. In the perfect world, even if total sales fluctuate and total cost of goods sold fluctuate, the gross profit margin itself should always remain relatively constant.

Watching expenses, dollar for dollar

You may be wondering what there is to understand when looking at expenses on a Profit & Loss report. After all, an expense is just an expense, isn't it? Well, maybe not quite. Keep two things in mind:

✔ Expenses are different from expenditure. *Expenditure* includes not just regular expenses, but also money spent on capital equipment. (You allocate capital expenditure to an asset account in the Balance Sheet, and not to an expense account in the Profit & Loss.) Therefore, while a Profit & Loss report shows all business expenses, it doesn't show all business expenditure.

✔ Unless you specifically request a cash-based Profit & Loss report, expenses show up in the Profit & Loss as soon as you record the bill, regardless of when you pay the supplier.

In addition to understanding how expenses appear on a Profit & Loss report, take action if the report itself looks like a dog's breakfast (there's nothing worse than a Profit & Loss report that lists pages of expenses in no particular order):

✔ If a business has a lot of expenses, group them into headings. Refer back to Figure 9-1, where I break down expenses into Administration Expenses, Occupancy Expenses and Payroll Expenses.

✔ Within each heading, keep expenses in alphabetical order. If you're using accounting software, you may need to re-number your expense accounts in order to get them to print in order.

✔ If you get an expense account with a piddly amount in it at the end of 12 months (less than $100 or so), get rid of it by combining this account with another similar expense account. The less clutter, the better.

✔ Calculating depreciation is usually a task that falls to the company accountant, and not the bookkeeper. If you're generating a draft Profit & Loss report for management to review, you may want to add a note that depreciation isn't included, and the profit may be overstated.

Painting a Picture with the Balance Sheet

A Profit & Loss report tells a story about what's going on in a business over any period of time. In contrast, a *Balance Sheet* is a candid snapshot of how much a business owns and how much it owes at any point in time.

In Figure 9-2, my sample Balance Sheet starts by listing assets (such as the bank account, inventory, shop fittings and so on), and then moves to liabilities (credit cards, trade creditors, loans and the like). The bottom line finishes with a flourish, calculating the difference between assets and liabilities. This figure represents the equity: the owner's or shareholders' stake in the business.

	This Year	Last Year	$ Difference	% Difference
Assets				
Current Assets				
Business Cheque Account	$18,782	$14,357	$4,425	31%
Petty Cash	$100	$100	$0	0%
Inventory	$50,800	$36,000	$14,800	41%
Trade Debtors	$10,440	$6,240	$4,200	67%
Total Current Assets	$80,122	$56,697	$23,425	41%
Non-Current Assets				
Shop Fitting at cost	$22,750	$21,500	$1,250	6%
Shop Fittings Accum Dep	-$9,260	-$4,000	-$5,260	-132%
Total Non-Current Assets	$13,490	$17,500	-$4,010	-23%
Total Assets	$93,612	$74,197	$19,415	26%
Liabilities				
Current Liabilities				
Visa Card	$1,500	$1,800	-$300	-17%
Trade Creditors	$9,790	$6,690	$3,100	46%
PAYG Withholdings Payable	$820	$520	$300	58%
Superannuation Payable	$1,372	$962	$410	43%
GST Collected	$12,439	$6,329	$6,110	97%
GST Paid	-$7,178	-$2,562	-$4,616	-180%
Total Current Liabilities	$18,744	$13,739	$5,005	36%
Non-Current Liabilities				
Bank Loans	$37,000	$22,000	$15,000	68%
Total Liabilities	$55,744	$35,739	$20,005	56%
Net Assets	**$37,868**	**$38,458**	**-$590**	**-2%**
Equity				
Owner's Capital Brought Forward	$38,458	$41,810	-$3,352	-9%
Less: Owners Drawings	-$49,060	-$55,010	$5,950	-12%
	-$10,602	-$13,200	$2,598	-25%
Current Year's Profits	$48,470	$51,658	-$3,188	15%
Closing Owner's Capital	**$37,868**	**$38,458**	**-$590**	**-6%**

Figure 9-2: A Balance Sheet provides a snapshot showing the assets and liabilities of a business.

If an auditor wants to check a set of accounts, their main tactic is usually to verify the balance of every single account in the Balance Sheet. (Why? Because if both the opening and the closing Balance Sheets for any given period are correct, the auditor can be sure the report that connects the two, namely the Profit & Loss report, is also correct.) As a bookkeeper, feel free to take a leaf out of the auditor's book and aim not only to understand every account on the Balance Sheet, but also be confident that the balance of every account is correct.

Sketching assets, black as ink

At first glance, understanding the assets section of a Balance Sheet is simple. Assets are just a list of what the business owns, right? Sure. But in order to make sure you understand the assets section of a Balance Sheet, you may want to dig a little deeper:

- ✔ A standard Balance Sheet starts by listing all bank accounts and cash balances. Easy to understand, but as a bookkeeper, you want to make sure that every single one of these balances is correct, up to date and matches with bank statements for the same period.

- ✔ Next on a Balance Sheet, also included in current assets (for definitions of current, non-current and intangible assets, refer to Chapter 2), you get Accounts Receivable and Stock on Hand. Your job is to check that Accounts Receivable matches against the Aged Receivables report, and that Stock on Hand matches against your inventory valuation report for that period.

- ✔ Non-current assets are next on the scene, shown at historical cost (in other words, the original cost of the asset) less depreciation. Beware that historical cost isn't necessarily a good indicator of what an asset is worth. Land and buildings in particular tend to increase in value over time, and historical cost doesn't reflect this.

- ✔ If you're doing a super-conscientious job, don't forget to compare the value of fixed assets on your Balance Sheet against the values on your depreciation schedule. (After all, isn't this a more worthy task than updating your Facebook status?)

- ✔ Intangible assets come last, and include assets such as company formation expenses, franchise purchase fees, goodwill, intellectual property and trademarks. With intangible assets, bear in mind that the value shown on the Balance Sheet doesn't necessarily reflect an asset's real worth. Goodwill in particular may be overstated or understated, as the value in the Balance Sheet usually only shows the amount a business paid for goodwill, and this payment could have been many years ago.

Opening balances and other headaches

If you're using accounting software, you may find that the Balance Sheet you generate doesn't match up with the Balance Sheet from your accountant. This discrepancy has two likely causes: Either you didn't set up opening balances correctly when you first installed the software, or you haven't adjusted your Balance Sheet to match the accountant's at year end (or maybe both!).

The best approach for setting up opening balances depends on the software you're using. Usually, you can't set up every opening balance straight away, because the company

accountant takes a few months to finalise accounts for the previous year. No worries — even if many months go by until you receive a Balance Sheet for the year just gone, you can still go back and complete your opening balances.

If the cause of your problem is that the accountant made adjustments to your previous year's figures, and you haven't yet brought the Balance Sheet into line with the accountant's, then you need to take a different tack. I talk more about year-end procedures in *Bookkeeping For Dummies*, Australia/ New Zealand edition.

Drawing liabilities, red as blood

Liabilities include everything that a business owes to others, such as credit card accounts, supplier bills, GST owing and bank loans. Make sure that you give the liabilities in your Balance Sheet the love they deserve:

- ✔ Make sure the balances of any credit cards equal credit card statements for the same period.

- ✔ Check out the balance of Accounts Payable and make sure this balance is the same as the Aged Payables report for the same period.

- ✔ Make sure any loans that appear in the Balance Sheet match with bank loan statements for the same period. You may also want to double-check the balances of any hire purchase accounts.

Sculpting equity, cast in gold

The *equity* section of a Balance Sheet represents the *interest* that
shareholders or owners have in the business, including both
capital contributed and the profit or loss built up over time. And,
as I explain in Chapter 3, because debits always equal credits,
total equity always equals the difference between assets and
liabilities.

If you're looking for a more intuitive understanding of equity,
maybe a real-life example will help. Imagine you pitch up in the
desert with two mates, Bruce and Wayne. You have ten bucks in
your pocket when you arrive. The state of play is

Assets $10   **Liabilities $0**   **Equity $10**

After a fabulous game of poker, you still have ten bucks but you
owe Bruce two dollars and Wayne owes you three dollars. You're
one dollar ahead! The state of play now is

Assets $13   **Liabilities $2**   **Equity $11**

In other words, you still only have $10 in your pocket, but the
equity in your noble poker business has increased. To calculate
equity, you add up all the assets (including things like cash,
customer accounts owing, motor vehicles and so on), and
then subtract all the liabilities (stuff like credit cards, supplier
accounts outstanding and loans).

The equity section of your Balance Sheet *always* equals the
difference between assets and liabilities. If total equity is a
positive figure, the business has made a profit over time and
some of this profit has been left in the business (either that, or
the business owners/shareholders have put their own capital
into the business). If total equity is a minus figure, that means
the business has made a loss over time or that business owners/
shareholders have taken out more than they have put in (or a
combination of both).

Understanding the Relationship between Profit and Cash

I can't believe how often clients ask, 'Veechi, my reports say I'm making heaps of profit, but how come there's nothing in the bank?' Similarly, I occasionally witness clients who are wallowing in cash and living the high life, even though their Profit & Loss reports are decidedly gloomy.

The long and short of it all — profit doesn't equal cash and cash doesn't equal profit.

Why there's profit but no cash

Why is it that sometimes a Profit & Loss report shows that a business is doing well but there's no cash anywhere to be seen? I set out a few possible explanations here:

- ✔ **The tax hounds have got in on the act:** The sad truth of the matter is that as soon as a business makes any profit, it has to pay tax. Tax payments chew up cash, but usually don't show on Profit & Loss reports (see the sidebar 'Where tax fits in' for more details).

- ✔ **The cash has gone towards buying new equipment:** Any new gear that costs more than a certain amount (between $100 and $1,000 depending on what tax concessions are available) isn't immediately tax-deductible and so doesn't show up as an expense on the Profit & Loss report, but gets listed as an asset instead.

- ✔ **The business has repaid loans:** Loan repayments don't usually show up as expenses, meaning that loan repayments gobble up cash but don't affect the profit.

- ✔ **Customers owe heaps of money:** If a business bills a customer in April, the Profit & Loss report shows this income in April, even though the business may not receive the cash until weeks or months later. If you look at the Profit & Loss report for the whole year and customers owe more at the end of the year than they did at the beginning, the difference is a direct drain on cash.

Where tax fits in

Business owners and bookkeepers often get confused about where income tax payments appear in a Profit & Loss report.

If a business has a sole trader or partnership structure, then any income tax payments are of a personal nature, and don't show up as an expense in the Profit & Loss, and instead get allocated to Owner's Drawings or Partner's Drawings. (If only I could claim my tax payments as a tax deduction, life would be that much sweeter ...)

If a business has a company structure, then income tax payments show at the very bottom of the Profit & Loss report, so that you have a total called Net Profit before Company Tax, followed by a total for Company Tax, then a final total called Net Profit after Company Tax.

Why there's cash but no profit

It may be easy to grasp why a business may not have any cash even though the business is turning a profit. However, what about the opposite scenario, where a business is rolling in cash but the Profit & Loss reports look decidedly gloomy? In many ways, this situation is even worse, because the business owner can all too easily get lulled into a false sense of security, spending beyond their means.

Here are some reasons why cash may be rosy but profit grim:

- ✔ **The business receives a loan:** Loans are both a blessing and a curse. When a business receives a loan, the sudden influx of cash can burn a hole in the thickest of pockets.

- ✔ **Creditors are building up:** A business can get by for quite a while making a loss but staying afloat, simply by running up outstanding accounts. If a business starts to stretch out suppliers to 60, 90 or even 120 days, it not only generates a fair amount of bad feeling, but wads of cash also.

- ✔ **Stock is running down:** If stock levels go down, the business has more cash available. Simple as that.

Reporting where cash came from, and where it went

When looking at cashflow, accountants sometimes refer to a *Statement of Cashflow*, a special report that examines the cashflows in and out of a business, and goes a long way towards explaining the mystery of why a business has a handsome profit, but no cash, or vice versa. Although fairly complex to assemble by hand, many accounting software packages offer this report as standard.

In Figure 9-3, I show a Statement of Cashflow report that connects the Profit & Loss report in Figure 9-1 with the Balance Sheet in Figure 9-2. The Difference column in the Balance Sheet shows how I arrive at the figures on this report. *Cash outflows* (cash going out of the business) show as negative amounts; *cash inflows* (cash coming in to the business) show as positive amounts.

The top section of my Statement of Cashflow report shows business operating activities used up $8,735 of cash, with $14,800 going to an increase in stock holdings. Investment activities show that new shop fittings chewed up $1,250 in cash, and financing activities show that the owner's personal drawings sucked up $49,060. The fact that the business had more cash in the bank at the end of the period than it did at the beginning is mainly attributable to the $15,000 bank loan it received.

Many people think that a cash-based Profit & Loss report does the same job as a Statement of Cashflow report. Not true. As you can see from Figure 9-3, a Statement of Cashflow includes a lot of information that you don't get on a cash-based Profit & Loss, such as details about bank loans, owner's drawings and new equipment purchases.

Statement of Cashflow
July 2009 through to June 2010

Net Profit			$ 48,469.80
Inventory	$	(14,800.00)	
Trade Debtors	$	(4,200.00)	
Shop Fittings Accum Dep	$	5,260.00	
Visa Card	$	(300.00)	
Trade Creditors	$	3,100.00	
PAYG Withholdings Payable	$	300.00	
Superannuation Payable	$	410.40	
GST Collected	$	6,110.00	
GST Paid	$	(4,615.60)	
Cashflows from Operating Activities			$ (8,735.20)
Net Cashflows from Operating Activities			$ 39,734.60
Shop Fitting at cost	$	(1,250.00)	
Net Cashflows from Investing Activities			$ (1,250.00)
Bank Loans	$	15,000.00	
Owners Drawings	$	(49,060.00)	
Net Cashflows from Financing Activities			$ (34,060.00)
Net Increase in Cash for the Period			$ 4,424.60
Cash at the Beginning of the Period	$	14,457.00	
Cash at the End of the period	$	18,881.60	
Difference in Cash			$ 4,424.60

Figure 9-3: A Statement of Cashflow explains the difference between profitability and cash in the bank.

The true nature of the beastie

Some businesses — especially small businesses — prefer to report on a cash basis. (In Chapter 3, I explain the difference between accrual and cash-basis accounting.)

When you're looking at a Profit & Loss report, make sure you know what it is that you're dealing with. Is this a cash or an accrual report? Remember, with *accrual accounting*, you recognise income at the time the sale occurs, regardless of when you receive cash from a customer.

With *cash accounting*, you recognise income only when you receive cash in your sticky hand. The same principle applies to expenses.

If you're looking at a Profit & Loss report on a cash basis, remember that this report may not reflect the true profitability of this business, especially if the business carries a lot of stock, owes significant amounts to suppliers or is owed heaps from customers.

Part IV
The Part of Tens

Glenn Lumsden

*'Bookkeeping? I love bookkeeping.
Bookkeeping is my life. In fact,
now that I've mentioned it three times
I can claim you as a deduction.'*

In this part . . .

The part of tens is my favourite part of any *For Dummies* title. Here is when I get to be short and snappy, and fire off instructions nineteen to the dozen. (Although my husband claims that I get to do this every morning, I beg to differ.)

In Chapter 10, I delight in sharing my basket of tricks for getting customers to pay on time, and I even manage to do so without mentioning martial arts, blackmail or enforced babysitting duties of triplet boys.

Chapter 10

Ten Tricks for Collecting Money

In This Chapter

▶ Knowing and loving your credit policy

▶ Chasing money without delay

▶ Getting on the phone and let those debtors know you care

▶ Tracking every call made, every promise received

▶ Following through on your threats

*O*ne of the trickier jobs that often falls to a bookkeeper is chasing money from overdue accounts. If you don't have an outgoing personality or you're not naturally an assertive person, then the process of phoning people up and demanding money can feel like something akin to torture.

This reticence quickly turns into a negative cycle, because the longer you leave a debt before you chase it, the more likely it is that the debtor won't pay. The secret to getting paid is to have clear credit terms and make contact with customers the moment they go beyond these.

I can't cure any innate shyness you may have, but in this chapter I do provide a lot of tricks about how to chase money. Good luck!

Draw Up a Credit Policy

If you're charged with chasing money from customers, then you want to have a set of rules that outlines the deal for any customer who receives credit. This document is called a *credit policy*, and, if such a policy doesn't yet exist, it may be your job to draft one.

The kinds of things that go in a credit policy depend on the business, but usually include

- ✔ **What's the fine print on the credit application?** All customers who receive credit must complete a credit application. Make sure this application includes full contact details for the business owners and at least two credit or trade references.

- ✔ **What are the trading terms you offer to customers?** You may be wise to tailor your trading terms to different customers. For example, if you sell to any of the large retail chains, you'll get hammered for generous terms and hideous discounts. However, you can still stick to offering 7-day or 14-day terms to the rest of your customer base.

- ✔ **How often do you send customer statements?** I suggest you send customer statements monthly if you offer 30-day terms, or fortnightly if you offer 7-or 14-day terms.

- ✔ **How soon do you chase customers for money after a bill falls due?** I talk about this topic more in the section 'Don't Waste a Moment' later in the chapter.

- ✔ **At what point does a debt go to a collection agency or other legal action?** This crunch point varies from business to business. Make sure the policy also states whether you need approval before initiating legal action.

- ✔ **What are the goals in terms of debt collection and accounts receivable ratios?** A good credit policy should include goals, so that a bookkeeper knows what to aim for. For example, a goal could be to have an average collection time of 45 days, or to have less than 2 per cent of the total debts outstanding in 90 days or more.

Consider a Romalpa Clause

A *Romalpa clause* is when you retain title to the goods you sell until a customer pays in full. For example, if you sell merchandise to a retail store and the retailer doesn't pay your account, having a Romalpa clause means you are entitled to walk into the store and remove any of your unsold merchandise, up to the value of the unpaid account.

Romalpa clauses can be difficult to enforce, and you're usually best to get your lawyer to draft a Romalpa clause for you. Your lawyer will probably advise that you include the Romalpa clause in your customer credit application form, and may even suggest that you also include this clause at the foot of every invoice. The customer must sign that they are aware that the clause exists and must agree that, if push comes to shove, you have permission to enter their premises to recover your goods.

Don't Waste a Moment

When a customer's account runs overdue, get on the phone straightaway. By overdue, I'm not talking about 60 days or 90 days. Start chasing as soon as an account is seven days overdue. The longer you leave a debt before chasing it, the more risk you run of not getting paid.

Dun & Bradstreet, one of the world's most respected organisations specialising in risk and debt collection, offers the following statistics as motivation for acting promptly:

- ✔ For debts that are one month overdue, an average of 6.2 per cent never pay.

- ✔ For debts that are three months overdue, an average of 26.4 per cent never pay.

- ✔ For debts that are six months overdue, an average of 42.2 per cent never pay.

In other words, your chances of getting paid fall dramatically every month you wait before initiating the debt collection process. So don't be soft, don't be nice, and don't waste a single moment ...

Calculate the Cost of Debts

Sometimes I come across business owners who begrudge the bookkeeper the time they spend chasing debts. This always surprises me, because not only does the business risk increased bad debts the longer they wait before chasing money, but slow-paying customers tie up valuable capital.

If you — or the business owner — have trouble getting fired up about the idea of debt collection, then think of it this way: Imagine your monthly sales are $30,000 and customers pay on average in 60 days. If you can reduce this average from 60 days to 45 days, then you generate an extra $15,000 of working capital for your business, interest-free!

Get On the Blower

When chasing overdue accounts, I find phone calls work infinitely better than a pile of reminder letters. Over the years I've refined my telephone technique down to a fine art, so here are a few tips, straight from the horse's mouth:

- ✔ **Be polite, cheerful and warm:** Get to know the person(s) responsible for accounts by their first name and make sure they know who you are too. Ask about their family, their holidays — build rapport. (Being friendly is a great way to elicit guilt.)

- ✔ **Aim high:** Don't beat about the bush. Start by asking 'whether the payment will be sent immediately'. If the answer is 'no', ask why not. Let the person talk, and don't interrupt them.

- ✔ **Offer solutions:** If someone genuinely can't pay immediately, don't wait for them to tell you when they can pay, but instead provide a solution. Start by saying something like 'how about 50 per cent this week and the balance in 14 days?' If the customer rejects this solution, have another (gentler) solution up your sleeve that you can suggest instead.

- ✔ **Don't be fobbed off by excuses:** If a customer has lost the invoice, email or fax them a copy within the hour. If the invoice 'is delayed in the system', ask the accounts person to investigate what stage the invoice is up to. Say you're going to call back the next day.

- ✔ **Ask for a commitment:** When somebody makes a vague comment such as, 'I'll be paying that bill next week', or 'I'll attend to your account as soon as possible', reply by saying: 'Thanks so much for that. Does this mean I can expect a payment by such-and-such a date?' If the customer agrees, confirm their response by saying: 'That's great. I'm writing in my diary to expect your payment by (say) 31 March. If I don't receive your payment by 1 April, I'll phone again to check there are no problems.'

> ✔ **Confirm commitments in writing:** If someone promises to pay by a certain date, send an email as soon as you hang up the phone thanking them for this commitment, and confirming the agreement they have just made.

Don't Give Too Many Options

If a customer is overdue with their account, avoid giving too many options when you chase money. For example, if you send reminder letters, don't ask that customers settle their accounts within 14 days. Instead, simply ask for immediate payment. After all, the customer is already overdue — why cut them any more slack?

Similarly, customise your statement format so that instead of having Current, 30 days, 60 days, 90 days and even 120 days plus as totals on the bottom of the statement, simply have two totals: Current and Overdue. You don't want to be sending the message that it's okay, or even possible, for someone to go 120 days over on their account.

Keep a Dossier

Keep track of every phone call made, every letter sent and every promise received. Sometimes it takes months, numerous phone calls and many letters before you succeed in getting someone to pay, and if you repeat this process with a lot of debtors, you soon lose track of who promised what.

How you log this activity depends on what systems you're using. If the accounting software permits, I like attaching notes to a customer contact log that not only documents all activity, but also allows me to flag re-contact dates. This function means that if a customer promises to pay by a certain date, I can note this date in the log, and then the software prompts me when this date rolls around.

An alternative is to maintain notes in a spreadsheet such as Excel. The flexibility of a spreadsheet means you can put notes in any format, but still be able to search or sort by customer name, amount or re-contact date.

Track 'em Down

What if you're chasing a debt and the customer isn't answering the phone, or the letters you send get returned? You may need to don your Sherlock Holmes hat and do some creative tracking:

- ✔ **Search online:** You can often find people simply by Googling their name. If this tactic doesn't work, try the white pages online at www.whitepages.com.au.

- ✔ **Use a professional:** If you have a relationship with a debt collection agency, you can request a Credit Reference report. Some agencies even provide a tracing service for 'lost debtors'.

- ✔ **Try local connections:** If you know that a debtor was living in rented premises, phone the local real estate agent and ask if they know where this person moved to. Alternatively, go to the street where that person lived, and knock on the neighbours' doors. (Just remember not to tell the neighbours why you're trying to find this person, otherwise you may fall foul of privacy laws.)

- ✔ **Contact the references on the initial credit application:** If you received a credit application from this debtor, check out the credit or trade references they supplied, and see if these people or companies know where this person is now.

Stick to the Law

Although I encourage you to be assertive and forthright when chasing money, you must be careful never to be rude, nor to chase money in a way that could be described as harassment. Here are some guidelines about where assertiveness ends and harassment begins:

- ✔ Don't phone debtors on a public holiday or after 9 pm at night.

- ✔ Never contravene privacy laws. If you can't get through to the person who owes you money, it's okay to leave a message saying that you called, but you mustn't say what your call is concerning.

- ✔ Don't make contact more than three times per week, or more than ten times per month. Contact includes speaking to the debtor (including if the debtor hangs up), letters, text messages, telephone messages or emails.

- ✔ Leave a reasonable amount of time between making each contact.

- ✔ If you're considering visiting the debtor's home, first seek advice from your lawyer regarding privacy and consumer protection laws.

- ✔ Never make any kind of physical threat.

- ✔ Don't make idle claims in your correspondence. For example, don't say 'numerous attempts have been made to contact you' if this isn't the case, and don't say 'you will be liable for collection charges and fees' if that isn't true.

For a more detailed summary about the rights and responsibilities of a debt collector, visit the ACCC website at www.accc.gov.au and download the free publication *Debt collection guideline for collectors and creditors: joint publication by ACCC and ASIC.*

Get Drastic

You may have been reading through all my debt-collection tips, thinking to yourself: 'She's optimistic. None of those strategies would work with so-and-so.' I agree. There are some people who are professional payment-avoiders. They know how to take you right to your limit and maybe beyond, and are quite content in the knowledge that some of their suppliers are likely to give up along the way, letting them get off, scot free.

So here's my strategy for getting blood out of the proverbial stone:

1. **Do all the basic stuff first.**

    Don't go in heavy straightaway, or you may lose a customer. Send statements, make phone calls and send at least one reminder letter. Be prepared to accept repayments in two or three instalments, if that helps.

2. **Decide what action you're prepared to take.**

    You may need to discuss with management how far they're prepared to take this matter. In warning a customer of what may occur, do you intend to issue a summons at the local court, or to refer this debt to a collection agency such as D&B (visit www.dnb.com.au for more details).

3. **Send a final warning letter, asking for immediate payment, and explaining what action you intend to take if payment isn't received.**

    When you realise that being nice isn't working, send a final letter of warning, seeking immediate payment. In this letter, explain what is going to happen if this deadline isn't met (a bit like dealing with kids, isn't it?).

    I suggest that you send final warning letters by registered post, so that there can be no doubt that this letter gets to its destination. Don't put your business name on the outside of the envelope (this avoids the risk of the debtor seeing the envelope, thinking 'Oh no, not them again', and turfing the envelope in the bin without even opening it).

4. **If seven days roll by without payment or contact by the debtor, then carry out your threat.**

    Whatever you threaten, you must be prepared to follow it through. If you threaten to take legal action, then send the lawyer's letter within a fortnight. If you threaten to cut off supply, then do so.

Index

Notes

. . . .

FOR DUMMIES®

Business & Investment

1-74216-971-6
$39.95

1-74216-853-1
$39.95

1-74216-852-3
$39.95

0-7314-0991-4
$39.95

1-74216-962-7
$19.95

0-7314-0828-4
$19.95

0-7314-0827-6
$19.95

1-74216-941-4
$36.95

1-74031-166-3
$39.95

0-7314-0724-5
$39.95

0-7314-0940-X
$39.95

1-74216-859-0
$32.95

FOR DUMMIES®

Reference

1-74216-972-4
$39.95

1-74216-945-7
$39.95

1-74031-157-4
$39.95

0-7314-0723-7
$34.95

Health & Fitness

1-74216-946-5
$39.95

0-7314-0760-1
$34.95

1-74216-984-8
$39.95

1-74031-011-X
$39.95

Technology

0-470-49743-2
$34.95

0-7314-0761-X
$39.95

0-7314-0941-8
$39.95

1-74031-159-0
$39.95